WOMEN OF VISION

Their Lives, Struggles, and Triumphs

Evangelist Mariah Landrum Childs

Publisher
Celestial Enterprises Unlimited, Inc.

23-2004

Gwendolyn —

Wait patiently
on the Lord — He has
heard your prayers

Mariah

CONTENTS

A WOMAN OF VISION

∞

Early in the morning,
Before I begin my day,
I pray to God for guidance,
As I journey on my way.

He never is too busy,
To listen to my prayers.
He directs and leads me…
In ways that show He cares.

I have had many dreams…
Which He has helped come true.
If you put your faith in Him-
He'll do the same for you.

Just strive to do His work,
And seek His perfect will…
And He will be right there-
Your visions to fulfill.

He's a God of Inspiration.
He will help expand your mind…
Your visions for the future,
He will fulfill in *His* own time.

Mariah Landrum Childs

DEDICATION

This book is dedicated to my beloved mother, Georgia I. Stringer Landrum, a virtuous woman, who constantly teaches me by her example what it means to be a woman of vision. Through her creativity and imagination, she has always been able to "take something that appeared to be of no significance and transform it into something of beauty."

ACKNOWLEDGEMENTS

First, all honor and glory goes to my Lord and Savior Jesus Christ who inspired me to collect the testimonies of these women of vision, and share them with the readers of this book.

Honor and thanks to my parents, Moses and Georgia Landrum, who gave me a solid foundation in the Christian faith, and encouraged me to pursue my passion for writing.

Special thanks to my children: Christopher, Jonathan, and Rebecca, who have faithfully stood with me through the good times and bad, and have traveled the many miles of my Christian journey with me.

Extra Special thanks to my son and brother in Christ, Christopher, who encouraged me to pursue my vision, and for his celestial editing.

Special thanks to my colleague and friend, Yvonne Warren, for her support and editing.

Special thanks to the members of the St. Philip Monumental AME Women of Vision Ministry for their prayers and devoted support.

Special thanks to my spiritual mother and friend, Shirley Dopson, who has counseled, prayed, and helped me in countless ways to face and walk through the many trials I encountered while in Savannah.

Special thanks and appreciation go to the following Women of Vision who boldly share their lives and testimonies, so that others may find strength, hope, and increased faith:

> Jeanette Bacon, Savannah GA
> Janice Cooper, Savannah, GA
> Laurie M. Craig, Halifax, MA
> Joy Cummings, Savannah GA
> Shirley D'Agostino, Brockton, MA
> Sharon Eswine, Savannah, GA,
> Vera Gardner, Savannah, GA
> Beverly Greene, Brockton, MA
> Beatrice Johnson, Savannah, GA
> Debra Johnson, Columbus, GA
> Lorraine Johnson, Randolph, MA
> Tammy A. K, Mixon, Savannah, GA
> Agatha Morris, Savannah, GA
> Linda Robinson, Savannah, GA
> Rev. Peola Scott, Savannah GA
> Kathy Tamulevich, Hanson, MA

PREFACE

"In all thy ways acknowledge Him, and He shall direct thy paths..." (Proverbs 3:6 NIV)

W ho are these women of vision? They are *God's handmaidens* I have encountered, spanning over more than twenty years as I've traveled on my Christian journey from Boston, Massachusetts to Savannah, Georgia. These women of vision are like a collection of fabric pieces found in a patchwork quilt. They are different in their ambitions, backgrounds, ages, and colors. However, there is a common thread that stitches them together. It is their love and commitment to Jesus Christ. God, the Master Quilter, strategically positioned each woman to be used as a vessel to assist me as I have walked down the road of my Christian experience. These women have powerful real life stories to share. As a result of them surrendering their wills and lives into the care of God, their lives have become transformed. These women have come to believe through their life experiences that God is faithful and that *nothing* is impossible for God.

On many occasions, these women have been faced, sometimes daily, by challenges in their health, relationships, finances, emotions, careers, and even in their spiritual relationships with God. Even when their life situations told them there was no possibility of having a positive outcome, these women of vision saw those things that were not as though they were. They believe according to Hebrews 11:1, "Now, faith is the substance of things hoped for, the evidence of things not seen." Sometimes they have had to persevere against wagging tongues, shut doors, and doubting family members and friends. Yet, they chose to boldly step out on faith and believe that Jesus Christ was their answer. Their confidence that He was advocating on their behalf daily with the Father was often all they had to hold on to. Yet, they continually put one foot in front of the other and rose up to face the obstacles that lay before them.

These women of vision accepted Jesus Christ as their personal Lord and Savior. They commit their lives to trust in the Lord with all their hearts in all their affairs. In each situation they face, whether positive or negative, they choose to worship, praise, and magnify the name of the Lord. These women are believers who dare to stand on the promises of God, and believe that He has a purpose and a preordained destiny for their lives.

Though each woman may have felt emotionally worn and cast away at some point in her life, the redeeming love of Christ and the tightly knotted bond of friendship, have given each one the fortitude to press on. In these pages, these women of vision share their personal testimonies and give the reader a glimpse into their lives. Their testimonies show how Jehovah met them at their point of need. In times of lack, He proves Himself faithful as Jehovah-Jireh. In times of physical challenge, He presents Himself as Jehovah-Ropheka, Jehovah that heals. In the midst of their storms, He sends peace and He presents Himself as Jehovah-Shalom. Their prayer is that someone feeling hopeless may be encouraged, and someone who is in need of a Savior, may be compelled to turn his or her heart towards Jesus Christ and accept Him as the Lord of their life. These women of vision share their stories, because they believe "They overcome him by the blood of the Lamb and by the word of their testimony." (Revelation 12:11 NIV)

INTRODUCTION

"Write the vision, and make it plain upon tables...For the vision is yet for an appointed time, but at the end it shall speak, and not lie: though it tarry, wait for it; because it will surely come, it will not tarry." (Habakkuk 2:2-3 KJV)

A *vision* according to the Application Study Bible (NIV) is "a supernatural revelation, including a dream, consisting of symbolic images, often accompanied by interpretations."

I am a witness of God's faithfulness to fulfill the visions He may give you through dreams. It may take time for the manifestation to take place, but you must be patient and wait for it. In 1986, the Lord gave me a vision through a dream that I distinctly remember. It has profoundly impacted my life. Because I journal on a regular basis, I wrote it down, so I would not forget it. I am glad I did, because now by sharing the vision, it can help strengthen the faith of others.

In the dream, I envisioned myself walking down a dusty red clay road. I was dressed in layered shades of brown sheer fabric that was draped around me from my head to my sandaled feet- in the style of women in ancient Israel. My face was veiled. On both sides of the road, there were women dressed in similar clothing. Each one had items in her hands which she was extending out for me to take. I remember that I felt I did not want to take anything that they were offering (in my former prideful I can handle it myself attitude). I was attempting to walk on without accepting anything when I suddenly heard a voice speak. It said, "I will provide handmaidens for you to help you with whatever you will need for your journey, but it will be up to you whether or not you will receive what they have to offer."

I can still remember feeling humbled and sorry for my arrogance. In the dream, my attitude seemed to change. I saw myself smiling and graciously accepting all the gifts that were being offered to me by the women. I then believed that God was actually providing the gifts and the *handmaidens* were His vessels. I never forgot that dream.

Now, I have a much clearer understanding of what the Holy Spirit was revealing to me in that vision. I realize that there have been many *handmaidens of God* who He has used as vessels to assist me along the course of my Christian journey. As I look back, I don't know how I would have made it through many of my struggles if it were not for their gifts of friendship, strength, encouragement, provision, and prayer which have made my journey so much easier.

Each *handmaiden* has impacted my life in a special and unique way. Some who were more spiritually *seasoned* imparted to me their spiritual wisdom, guidance and counsel. Others shared with me their gifts of creativity and helps. Still others opened their homes to me when I needed refuge, helped care for my children, provided job opportunities, and even provided basic needs such as groceries when my cupboards were almost bare. I have always stood on God's Word, "Never have I seen the righteous forsaken or their children begging bread." (Psalm 37:25 NIV) He has never failed me!

The greatest gift that I continue to receive from these *handmaidens of God* is their faithful prayers. Though thousands of miles separate some of us, there is no distance in time or space with prayer. Because God joined us together by His Spirit, He periodically places me on their hearts when I am going through a trial, and they intercede for me through prayer. Because God is reciprocal, He does the same with me for each of them, and I prayerfully intercede on their behalves. When we finally get the opportunity to talk to one another, we are always amazed that we knew just when and often exactly what to pray for one another. "The prayer of a righteous man is powerful and effective." (James 5:16 NIV)

The vision described, above which God blessed me with seventeen years ago, has been fulfilled time and time again. God has faithfully provided for everything I have needed thus far on my Christian journey: spiritually, emotionally, financially and physically. Many times God has allowed for my needs to be met through these *handmaidens* whom He has strategically placed in my path to help me along my way— just as He revealed to me in the dream. These *handmaidens* are women of vision as well, committed to serve and worship Jehovah God. Their testimonies are shared in these pages to encourage and strengthen the reader's faith.

This book is written for those who have chosen to live a life for Christ, and for those who do not know Him as their personal Lord and Savior, or have not fully surrendered their lives into His care...yet! There are many things that happen to all of us in life that we can't fix, can't escape, and simply must go through. God has promised to be with us in the valley or on mountain top experiences in our lives and never to abandon or leave us. Sometimes you may feel that no one has gone through what you have, and your situation is far worse than anyone else's. This is not true. According to I Corinthians 10:13. "No temptation has seized you except what is common to man. And God is faithful, He will not let you be tempted beyond what you can bear. But when you are tempted, He will also provide a way out, so you can stand up under it."

Being a woman of vision may sometimes cause you to look foolish in the eyes of others. However, just continue to hold on to your vision by faith, and be courageous enough to believe in the invisible, and expect the impossible. "For with God nothing shall be impossible." (Luke 1:37 KJV) Through the years, I have learned that God works in mysterious ways, and He may not come exactly *how* or *when* you may think He should, but He is always on time. I give all honor and glory to my Lord and Savior Jesus Christ for blessing me to see those things that are not as though they are.

Reading these testimonies will give you hope and confidence to believe that if God delivered, healed and blessed these women, He *can* and *will* do the same for you! God is no respecter of persons. "And Peter opened his mouth and said, 'Most certainly and thoroughly I now perceive *and* understand that God shows no partiality and is no respector of persons.'" (Acts 10:34 Amp.) Your faith will be strengthened, and you will be encouraged to think back and remember what God has done for you. Hopefully, you will be inspired, and motivated to share your personal testimony as an encouragement for someone else.

"The road of righteousness is never smooth nor soft
For those who choose to walk it.
But there are blessings hidden within each rough part,
If you just take the time to find them."

D. Christopher Lake

Chapter 1

TESTIMONIES OF DELAY

"They that wait upon the Lord shall renew their strength; they shall mount up with wings as eagles; they shall run, and not be weary, *and* they shall walk and not faint."
(Isaiah 40:31 KJV)

I married when I was twenty-two years old, after I had graduated from college. Things seemed to be going according to *my* envisioned schedule: I was engaged in my senior year of college and married the summer I graduated. My husband was finishing up his college education, and had not been drafted into the Army much to my delight. I was working on a job in my field of study-life was great! Then things began to lead me down a path I had not prepared for.

My husband and I (more so he) had decided to delay having children. Initially, this seemed like a *good* thing, because we would have time to save and just be with each other. After about the first year, however, *Mother Nature* started to *kick in*. I began to have the *yearning* to have a child. This came as an unforeseen surprise to me. My life had been going along pretty much according to *my* plan until this yearning began. What was this growing desire to have a baby? Hadn't I agreed with my husband to wait at least five years?

Most of my friends had gotten married around the same time I did. Many of them suddenly started to have children. Initially, I was an enthusiastic participant in baby showers, baby shopping sprees, and name selections. However, as time went on, it became increasingly more difficult to wear the mask of complacency. Oh for sure, I was sincerely happy for my friends and I never coveted their pregnancies or the children when they arrived. I was right there with gifts and helping out where I could. Only when I returned to our house, would I allow myself to feel the *ache* of being childless.

I involved myself in a lot of things to help sublimate my agony—taking art classes, traveling to Europe, sewing, etc. These distractions would last for a *season*, but the desire to have a child just seemed to return with a *vengeance*. It grew more and more difficult to see pregnant women or be around newborn babies. I would wear the mask of "Oh, we have decided to wait a while longer" when all the time, I knew I wanted to be a mother more than anything else in the world.

Finally, my *sentence* was lifted. I could stop using birth control. I was ecstatic! Little did I know that just because *we* had decided to try to get pregnant did not mean that it would happen right away. All I knew was that I had, in my opinion, *suffered* long enough. So we began trying to conceive. Month after month I hoped that my period would not come, but just like clockwork it would appear. After several months of trying and weeping, I began to think that maybe something was wrong with us. Maybe we *couldn't* get pregnant. That thought had never occurred to me, because all my other friends had no trouble. I was in good health, and regular. So what was the problem?

My mother and friends told me to relax, and that I was getting too uptight about the whole thing. This only made me become more frustrated. Soon I stopped talking about it to anyone, because they just didn't *understand* how I felt. Only I could feel the emptiness within my womb.

I had attended church regularly all my life, and had prayed daily. In my despair, I turned to God who had been faithful to help me in so many areas of my life in the past. My hope and faith in God hearing and answering my prayers was the only thing that seemed to keep me going.

Because I have always been an impatient person, waiting was *never* something I could do easily, especially when it was something I *really* wanted. However, I learned *patience* through this experience. I remembered someone quoting James 1:2-3, "Consider it pure joy, my brothers, whenever you face trials of many kinds, because you know that the testing of your faith develops perseverance." I thought to myself, "This certainly seems to apply to me, but *how long Lord?*"

Finally, we decided to seek infertility help. I wanted to know if there really was something wrong. The tests showed that there was no problem. We were advised to try monitoring my time of ovulation. This method became even more frustrating and stressful than just trying the normal course especially since the results were the same—no conception—no baby!

We had lived in the first floor apartment in a three-family house, for over five years, so we decided to buy a home of our own. So I began busily searching for a house. This distraction took my mind off *babymaking* for a while. I found a house that I really liked. We put in a bid, and then my husband changed his mind. I was devastated. All my energy had been focused on house hunting. Now that that was over, my thoughts propelled me full speed again to my childless condition. No matter how much I *pleaded* with God or tried to be good, I did not conceive.

Then, one night when I was ever so weary, I remember my husband wanting to be intimate. That was the last thing on my mind, and I began drifting off to sleep. I thought I had *dreamed* we made passionate love, and never gave it a second thought. To my surprise, however, my period did not come that month. Initially, I did not even think that I might be pregnant. After a week or so, I mentioned it to a close friend who suggested that I should I get a pregnancy test at the clinic where I was working at the time. I told her that I would think about it. Secretly, I was too afraid that I might not hear what I had waited to hear for six long years. Finally, when another week passed by, I knew something must be up, because I was always so regular, and my breasts began to feel tender and tingle.

Finally, I got up enough courage to have the pregnancy test done. I did not have it done where I worked, because I didn't want anyone to know I was still trying. I made an appointment and went in to my healthcare provider and took the test. They told me they would call me with the results later that day. When I received a call at work, I didn't think anything of it until I heard the voice on the other end of the telephone say, "Congratulations, you are going to be a mother." These were the words I had been waiting to hear for so *very* long. Tears began to fill up in my eyes, and my heart started racing.

"A what?" I asked the nurse, "Are you sure?"

She confirmed my questions, "Yes, you *are* pregnant. You *are* going to be a mother."

I hung the phone up in a daze and sat down in the chair that was nearby. I thought, "Oh, God, you did not forget about me. You did hear my prayers. You have given me the desire of my heart." Eight months later we were blessed with a seven pound -fourteen ounce baby boy. As I held him tenderly in my arms, I could hardly believe he was mine. At long last, after waiting seven *long* years, I was finally a mother.

The number "seven" is God's number for completion. "And by the seventh day God had finished the work He had been doing; so on the seventh day He rested from all His work. And God blessed the seventh day and made it holy, because on it He rested from all the work of creating that He had done." (Genesis 2:2-3 NIV) So too, did I rest on August 2, 1974, when my labor of childbirth was finished, and my first born son was nestled in my arms.

"Where there is no vision the people perish."
(Proverbs 29:18 KJV)

I am a married mother of three sons. Two are in their twenties, and my youngest is eight years old. For over twenty years I have taught Middle School in the Public School System. The Lord has given me a heart to work with students who are slow learners. Over the years, they have taught me patience, tolerance, and the ability to accept them unconditionally regardless of their ability or temperament. Perhaps, this is because as a child I was very shy and found it difficult to speak up. However the Holy Spirit changed that when I accepted Christ as my personal Lord and Savior. He has given me the skill to deal with people from all walks of life with Holy Ghost boldness and wisdom.

I have come to realize that the Lord has blessed me with the ability to negotiate. Through this gift, I have been able to overcome many obstacles in my life and have been able to help family members resolve problems with creditors and medical institutions. The Holy Spirit seems to just guide me to the right person at the right time, and then gives me the perfect things to say to help resolve the problem. Sometimes, I cannot believe that the words are coming from *my* mouth. Remarkably, they usually bring about positive resolutions. "But when he, the Spirit of truth comes, he will guide you into all truth. He will not speak on his own; but will speak only what he hears, and he will tell you what is yet to come."

(Corinthians 16: 13 NIV)

About ten years ago, the Lord gave me a vision to develop an organization that would combine my negotiating and teaching skills to teach mothers, grandmothers and women with limited resources who care for children, how to become better advocates for themselves and their children. The goal of the organization would be to help empower these women who may feel powerless to learn how to negotiate with the various environmental systems that they must deal with. Learning better life skills would help them become able to provide a better way of life for themselves and their families.

A "poverty mentality" is a demonic spirit that often hinders women from receiving all that they are entitled to, because they do not feel entitled to a better way of life. It can also hinder them from attaining the life skills they need to resolve conflicts and avoid domestic violence.

Through this organization, women will be mentored in the areas of Christian discipleship, life skills, the use of prayer, and developing confidence in God's ability to help them overcome the challenges they face in their lives.

Though I was given this vision to help women confront poverty many years ago, it has not been fully realized yet. However, over the years, I believe that God has been equipping and preparing me for what I perceive will be a ministry by allowing me to go through various situations and trials in my own life. These challenges have given me first hand knowledge of how many of the world's systems work and how to effectively maneuver within them. I have learned how situations that may seem to be impossible get resolved with God's help. I have also learned that when God gives you a vision it may take a long time before it comes into full manifestation. Though it has been delayed, I know I must hold on to the vision. I believe when God's appointed time has come; it will be fulfilled.

Chapter 2

TESTIMONIES OF REDEMPTION

"For God so loved the world that He gave His one and only Son, that whosoever believes in Him shall not perish, but have everlasting life." (John 3:16 NIV)

In 1999, I was divorced for the second time after fifteen years of marriage. My first marriage lasted ten years, so I was no stranger to either marriage or divorce.

During my second marriage, I experienced days filled with happiness and joy. Yet, there were days filled with hurt, anger and disappointment causing me to question why I had ever remarried.

My second divorce, on one hand had seemed to be an end of turbulence, conflict, and emotional pain. However, that was an illusion. For when my husband divorced me, he also divorced himself from our children: a son who was fifteen and a daughter who was just entering her teen years. Any sense of relief I may have felt was diminished by having to cope with my children's shock, anger, and deep sense of loss and emotional pain. In all honesty, I cannot say that I did not shed tears of grief myself, because I did. I also felt a deep sense of shame and guilt that here I was again faced with being left alone and abandoned by my husband.

I distanced myself from my in-laws, and they withdrew themselves from the children and me. I felt betrayed by my husband's infidelity, lies and deceit. But most of all, I was angry that he had not only walked away from me, but he had also walked away from our children who had always had a loving and close relationship with him. The more he withheld himself from them by making himself unavailable, the angrier I became. Oh, yes, to be sure I was also personally angry and hurt that he had left me, too. For a brief season, he left me *holding the bag*, and putting the total responsibility of caring and providing for the children on me, so he could "do his own thing"! I was living thousands of miles away from my homeland feeling frustrated, angry, and alone. What kept me going was the knowledge that my children *needed* me, and believing that God was with us and would not desert us. I clung to the Word, and meditated daily on (Isaiah 54: 4-6 NIV) "Do not be afraid; you will not suffer shame. Do not fear disgrace; you will not be humiliated. You will forget the shame of your youth and remember no more the reproach of your widowhood. For your Maker is your husband-the Lord Almighty is His name-the Holy One of Israel is your Redeemer, He is called the God of all the earth. The Lord will call you back as if you were a wife deserted and distressed in spirit- a wife who married young, only to be rejected," says God.

To be honest, my husband had initially told me that we should wait before we got married, because he did not have his life situated to care for a wife. Oh, but I was *so* in love and *so* determined that together we could make it. Besides, we had lived together for a couple years before we married, and I was feeling overwhelming guilt and shame. Living together before we were married caused my mother, who was a devout Christian, to distance herself from me. She stopped calling or coming to my home. This really hurt and pierced my spirit, because we had always been close, and I wanted her approval. (At this time *my own desires* had blinded me from realizing I was sinning before my eight year-old son). Yet, more than anyone else, I was offending God.

During this time, of growing conviction, I attended an evangelistic crusade during a spring break from the local college where I was teaching at the time. I had two weeks off, and I kept going back— day and night! I was hungry for the Word and the mind changing teaching about spiritual warfare and deliverance. Finally, on the third day, I could resist no longer the wooing of the Holy Spirit. I tearfully surrendered my will and my life into the hands of God, and I got saved!

After my conversion, I was convicted and determined to live holy. I decided I had to turn away from my rebellious lifestyle that had really stemmed from the hurt and disappointment I felt from my first failed marriage. In an attempt to eliminate my emotional pain and to show my displeasure towards God for not preventing my first marriage from failing, I allowed my hurt and neediness to draw me into an ungodly alliance with my boyfriend. Though we were not married, we lived together for two years. After my conversion, I told my boyfriend (who God had conveniently allowed to be out of the state attending a conference) that we could no longer live together in sin. I told him that while he was gone I'd gotten saved, and I had decided to follow Jesus, and I was not turning back! I convinced him to go to the crusade, and *he* got saved too! We were married seven days later with all the trimmings. Now, I could not believe that after *all* that we had been through, the marriage was really over.

Because of the divorce and the feeling of abandonment, our son was very angry and in a great deal of emotional pain. He took a lot of it out on me—temper tantrums, defiance, and disobedience (but only within the home) thank God! He would have nothing to do with his father for a very long time. He accepted no phone calls or visits from his father. I spent a lot of time shedding tears and praying. I believed that "Weeping may endure for a night, but joy cometh in the morning." (Psalm 30:5b KJV). I needed my morning to hurry up and come!

I began attending a noontime midweek church service, called Hour of Power at St. Philip Monumental AME Church where I shed what seemed to be endless tears. However, it was there that I was revitalized by the power of the Word that was delivered by the dynamic young pastor who preached with eloquence and force. On one occasion, recognizing my grief, the pastor ministered to me, gave me this scripture, and told me to meditate on it. The scripture says, "Forgetting those things which are behind, and reaching forth unto those things which are before, I press toward the mark for the prize of the high calling of God in Christ Jesus." (Philippians 3:13 KJV)

Since I am an avid quilter, I was inspired to design a *Scripture Quilt*. I embroidered the above scripture on it using batik fabric I had purchased that summer while I was in Africa. After finishing it, I proudly showed it to my father, who had always been a source of emotional comfort for me, just before he passed away in December 1999. His death left me feeling even more alone. I did not have his loving smile or words of comfort to help me through this valley experience. However, I did still have the Word and the gift of faith in Jesus Christ that he and my mother had imparted to me when I was very young.

That quilt and the scripture embroidered on it provided me with a sense of comfort and hope. I slept under that Word nightly for over three years. Slowly, I began to *live out* that scripture in my life. One day at a time I slowly began to forget my deep sense of anger, pain and disappointment. I moved on with my life, focusing on God and doing the work of the ministry to which God had called me.

I realize now that that scripture was a prophetic Word for my family and me. Through the grace and mercy of God, we have all moved on... My children and I have been healed in our spirits and emotions from the painful affects of the divorce. The Lord restored the relationships between the children and their father, his family, and me. My youngest son entered college in Atlanta, GA, the fall of 2002, and has done well academically, socially, and spiritually. My daughter continues to excel in school, does community service, works a part-time job, and has a powerfully anointed liturgical and step dance ministry at our church. My oldest son from my first marriage, remained faithful to the Lord, and was blessed with a beautiful Christian wife with a gentle and submitted spirit. They have been blessed with a new home in Atlanta, and have blessed me with my beloved first granddaughter.

The Lord *led* my children and me to become members of St. Philip Monumental AME Church, the place where God *hid me as* He *healed me*. There, He had me publicly accept my high calling as an evangelist. I preached my trial sermon there March 24, 2002 before my family and friends.

The Lord had *called* me as an evangelist when I was first saved March 1983. After a twenty year delay, (God was waiting for me to get myself ready, and He's not finished with me yet) I am actively serving on the ministerial staff at Monumental. I am also leading a

Bible study fellowship there where women gain support and victory as they face life's challenges by finding Godly solutions through study of the scriptures, prayer, and fellowship. The most remarkable thing is that now *I* deliver the Word often during the midweek Hour of Power Service. I find no greater joy than to encourage and lead men, women, and young people into the saving knowledge of Jesus Christ, and to see them accept *Him* as their Lord and Savior.

If God could *forgive*, *cleanse*, and then *use* a sinner like me for His glory, He *can* and *will* do the same for you! "And we know that in all things God works for the good of those who love Him, who have been called according to His purpose." (Romans 8:28 NIV)

"Therefore, I urge you brothers, in view of God's mercy, to offer your bodies as living sacrifices, holy and pleasing to God-this is your spiritual act of worship. Do not conform any longer to the pattern of this world, but be transformed by the renewing of your mind." (Romans 12:2 NIV)

WOMAN

I was a woman; born in shame; had no name, who to blame, all looked the same.

I was a woman; only ten, that man touched me again, tried to pretend, said he was my friend.

I was a woman; lonely and scared, nobody cared, rumors were smeared, it was what they feared.

I was a woman; said I was fast, aspersions were cast, reputations will last, mocked by my past.

I was a woman; fell in love with a man, just quicksand, tried to stand, stretched forth my hand.

I was a woman; battered and abused, victimized and accused, emotions were bruised, continued to be used.

I was a woman; tried to fight, never worked out all right, troubles in sight, bleak with my plight.

I was a woman; Christ came in my life, gave me new sight, said I'd be all right, don't stop the fight.

I am a woman; broke down that wall, started to crawl, after my fall, now I stand tall.

I am a woman; beautiful and true, strong because of what I've been through, just like brand new, let me help you.

"Fear not for I have redeemed you; I have summoned you by name; you are mine." (Isaiah 4:1)

I was gripped by a darkness that enclosed me like a cloth sack with a drawstring tied tight. I was suffocating and felt trapped. Here I was— a twenty-eight year old mother of three children who had married at sixteen and now was in my last semester of graduate school. The marriage was like a noose around my neck. Completing college was the driving force that kept me going, and even that began to feel like a cement block tied around my neck!

It was Christmas break, and I tried to muster up energy. No matter how hard I tried, I found myself sinking into what felt like a bottomless pit.

I had been in therapy for a year, and somewhere along the way my therapist had prescribed Valium to help relieve my anxiety. I started out sparingly, adhering to the prescribed dosage, but as time went on it became my constant *companion. She* put me to sleep at night, and woke me up in the morning. *She* was so easy to rely on, because *she* was always available and there were no questions asked. As time went on, I found myself depending on *her* even if I anticipated a problem or wanted to avoid any discomfort.

When pain and emptiness become a regular part of your existence, it's so easy to reach out for whatever provides relief. Some use food, sex, alcohol, shopping, or pills, and still there is no peace!

I found myself so busy spinning from one thing to another. I was *addicted* to being a caretaker—a rescuer. I never realized that vicariously I was trying to do for others what I so disparately needed for myself. I couldn't even see the flashing lights that warned of danger.

My plight was like the bleak, cold winter days, with the foliage stripped bare and limbs breaking from the weight of the elements. The place I resided was void of warmth. The sun no longer shined.

The turning point came when I took an overdose of pills. What if I died? I didn't want to die. I was trapped and saw no way out.

I was admitted to a psychiatric ward and stayed there three weeks. As I look back now, I realize that I was in a lot more trouble than I thought. I was drowning and did not know how to save myself. How was I going to let someone *in* when I didn't know how to trust? Being an incest survivor, my fate was sealed a long time ago.

I was afraid to sleep while at the hospital because my roommate *looked* crazy. She wanted to kill herself, because of her unresolved guilt over a boyfriend's death. As time went on, I realized we were more alike than different, for I too had unresolved guilt and unforgiveness inside.

I am an incest survivor, and because it involved family members that I loved, it forced me into a shameful place that told me something was wrong with *me*. Many incest survivors carry feelings of guilt and shame.

In my discharge meeting, the psychiatrist told me I was working hard, but on the wrong things. I was trying to protect myself, and didn't know how to be close to people. Unless I was care taking or trying to rescue, I didn't know where I fit.

When adults use children for their own pleasure, they teach them to deny themselves, and become a vehicle for someone else's pleasure. I was trying to keep myself protected. The problem was that this defense helped me to survive throughout my childhood, but now as an adult, in a different season of my life, the things I had used to protect me were now destroying me! I felt like I was stripped naked and thrown into the woods and told to find my way out.

I was invited to attend church with a friend. We sat up in the balcony—a nice safe place. As the minister spoke, it was as if he was speaking directly to me. The inner turmoil and desperation were exposed. He spoke of a God and the sacrifice that He made to set us free by sacrificing his only Son. I heard He wanted to have a personal relationship with me, and that He was a healer-a source of strength. Before I realized it, I was on my feet moving to the altar. I felt like something was *drawing* me. At the altar, I completely surrendered all my fears, my anxiety, my guilt and shame. My life has never been the same!

I came to know Jesus as my personal Savior. I developed a *hunger* and *thirst* to know more about Him. He was so real, and no matter what I was going through- I knew He would never leave or forsake me. When depression tried to creep back in, I was able to resist its grip because God had said in His Word that I *had* the victory, and if I resisted the devil he would flee. I stood on His Word and it became a part of my life. He said He would renew my mind. "Be transformed by the renewing of your mind." (Romans 12:2 NIV). This meant I had to think differently which also meant I had to learn more of His Word, and allow it to change my perspective. I cannot tell you my change came overnight; it is a process that is still unfolding. However, I have been freed from guilt and shame, and I am being renewed continuously.

Isaiah 61:1-3 is one of my favorite scriptures. "The Lord anointed me to preach the good news to the poor. He has sent me to bind up the brokenhearted, to proclaim freedom for the captives and release from darkness for prisoners, to proclaim the year of the Lord's favor and the day of vengeance of our God, to comfort all who mourn and provide for all who grieve in Zion-to bestow on them a crown of beauty for ashes, the oil of gladness instead of mourning, and a garment of praise instead of a spirit of despair. They will be called oaks of righteousness, planting of the Lord for a display of His splendor" (NIV)

"In You, O Lord, I have taken refuge;" (Psalm 71:1)

LOVE'S EMBRACE

I live as He gives me the breath that I breathe.
I sing with the voice that He fashioned for me.
I am in the present as He gives me life.
No longer my own, I've been bought with a price.

Arms He outstretched embracing the tree
Now in the Spirit reach out to hold me.
Arms never tired or weary in strife
But warm in their comfort, abundant in life.

So where will I run when the troubles arise?
I hold fast my stance and look to His eyes.
Filled with compassion and mercy and grace
I find I am strengthened to finish the race.

Surrounded by people of varying types
The hurts and the sorrows cut deep as a knife.
In Him are they healed, in my Lord alone,
Are the hardest of heartaches like pulverized stone.

Embracing the cares and the burdens of life
Each struggle and snaggle of being a wife,
A mother, a daughter, a sister, a friend,
The stalwart of family who stays to the end.

All this can I do as I am in His will.
Surrendering all, every pain, woe and ill
To the love that He bears with the tenderest touch
To fill me with peace as He covers the rough.

The edges too sharp that would do me great harm
No longer a threat when I rest in His arm.
Beauty for ashes, a pearl of great price,
A gift to the world is the pure love of Christ.

To God be the glory and honor, Amen.

"Do not think of yourself more highly than you ought, but rather think of yourself with sober judgement; in accordance with the measure of faith that God has given you. Just as each of us has one body with many members, and these members do not all have the same function, so in Christ we who are many form one body, and each member belongs to all the others. We have different gifts according to the grace given us."
(Romans 12:3-6b NIV)

THE GARDEN

Looking back on my spiritual path can be both instructive and renewing. Lately however, I have felt *led* to also look ahead, down the path. What does God have in store for me? Why does he work so hard to refine me? As I have prayed with these questions on my heart, God has *answered* me with a vision that is in an allegory.

I see a garden. In the garden, there is a good Gardener. He is humbly dressed, and as I look at Him, the sun obscures His face. The Gardener stands tall and appears to be able to view the entire garden with one glance. He knows the plan and timing for each aspect of the garden. My vantage point in the garden is low, close to the earth, because I am among the tools.

All around me are other tools—each with its own purpose. Some are well used; others less so, but all are useful. Many of the tools do not perceive their own shapes or "toolness" until the

Gardener has used them several times. Additionally, in this garden, a tool's shape and purpose may change over time as it allows itself to be useful to the Gardener. Most of the tools suffer from *pride* of one sort or another. It is a continual challenge among well-used tools not to get caught up in the admiration of the other tools, especially, when the others perceive the *honor* that *usefulness* bestows.

Frequently, tools try to direct the Gardener in His work. They may have been involved with the successful cultivation of many seeds in the garden, so they must constantly battle the feeling of pride within themselves believing that the ways of the Gardener and His work are no longer secret.

Sometimes tools even question the Gardener's use of them. One gasps, "But You are digging a hole with me."

"That's because you are a shovel," He says.

Luke 17: 7-10 speaks to this allegory: "Suppose one of you had a servant plowing or looking after the sheep. Would he say to the servant when he comes in from the field, 'Come along now and sit down to eat'? Would he not say, 'Prepare my supper, get yourself ready and wait on me while I eat and drink; after that you may eat and drink'?"

Would he thank the servant because he did what he was told to do? So you also, when you have done everything you were told to do, should say, 'We are unworthy servants; we have only done our duty.'"

For me this parable that Jesus spoke to His disciples has become instruction to those of us within the fold. When we have accomplished a task for God, what then?

"Maintain the servant spirit," comes as my answer. I realize for now I am but a shovel. However, I humbly accept my role and the tasks that are designed for me. In my walk of faith, I have learned that the Gardner knows best how and when my talents can best be used in helping complete His overall design.

"Jesus answered, 'I tell you the truth, no one can see the kingdom of God unless he is born again...born of water and the Spirit. Flesh gives birth to flesh, but the Spirit gives birth to the spirit. You should not be surprised at my saying,'
'You must be born again.' " (John 3:3-8 NIV)

I have been born again and filled with the Holy Spirit since 1973—over thirty years. I just thank God for saving me, and bringing me out of the world of sin. Yet, like so many others, I was in church from a child. I came from an Episcopal and Catholic background, and at that time I did not know or understand the things of the *Spirit*. I did not know what it meant to be *born again*. Thank God that the Lord sees our hearts, and knows what He has created each one of us to be. It may take some of us longer than others to recognize that we are not our own and have been *bought* with a price- the death of Christ on the cross. Today, I thank God for His mercy and grace and for choosing me before the foundations of the earth to serve Him.

I did not start my life out serving God. Oh, I was a *free* spirit! I did anything I was bold enough to do. But one day the Holy Ghost convicted me that I had to turn away from the life I was living because He had a greater purpose for my life. Initially, I did not know what it would be, but my desire to learn more about Him and to obey His scriptures grew inside my spirit more and more as I studied His Word.

Today, I know I have an evangelistic and prophetic *calling,* and God has used me mightily in this city. He used my natural outgoing nature to be *bold* for Christ. For many years I have worked in the prisons and on the streets witnessing the love of Jesus by reaching out to the lost and hurting throughout the community. I have extended words of encouragement and invitations to the lost to accept Jesus as their personal Lord and Savior.

Though I am a servant of the Lord, I have been through quite a bit, and I am *still* going through trials as a Christian wife and mother. The Bible tells us that when you have done all you can; just stand. "Therefore, my dear brothers, stand firm. Let nothing move you. Always give yourselves fully to the work of the Lord; because you know that your labor in the Lord is not in vain." (I Corinthians 15:58 NIV)

I am *still standing* and trying to encourage women to *hold on.* Marriage is not easy for Christian women. The enemy really wants to and does attack the family. He may make us believe it is our husband, or our children or other family members, but it is *him.* The Bible tells us, "For our struggle is not against flesh and blood, but against the rulers, against the authorities, against the powers of this dark world and against the spiritual forces of evil in the heavenly realms. Therefore put on the full armor of God, so that when the day of evil comes, you may be able to stand your ground, and after you have done everything, to stand." (Ephesians 6: 12-13 NIV) I try to encourage Christian women whose husbands may not be the *priests* of their homes like they ought to be (yet they profess Christ) that they must take on the role of *watchman* and stand in the gap for their family. Someone *must* do that in order to save the family, and to bring the loved ones into the kingdom of Christ.

I *know* that spiritual warfare is a very important realm of the Holy Spirit. God, in these last days, is calling men and women to *true* repentance and Godly sorrow. They are to be cleansed by the Blood of Jesus, and to *really* live holy for Him. Time is short! God is coming back for a remnant without *spot* or *wrinkle.*

It behooves all of us to be *broken* before God and consecrated, so that we can be used as tools in these end times, and so that the anointing of God can flow through us mightily. When we enter anywhere the anointing should have the *power* to make things change. In order for that to happen, we will have to *consecrate ourselves* and be *broken* before Almighty God.

I just thank God for this opportunity to share a little part of my testimony. I give all honor, glory and praise to Jesus Christ.

Chapter 3

TESTIMONIES OF HEALING

"With the stripes that wounded Him we are healed and made whole." (Isaiah 53:5 Amp.)

Would this excruciating pain inside my head disappear? I was unable to sit still. The pressure was intense. The prescribed pain-killers had not been effective, and the aggravating pain continued. When I decided to ask my husband to take me to the Emergency Room, I knew I was in trouble.

I had been unable to go to work, and that same morning I had found it difficult to get my girls off to school properly. Their supper remained unprepared, because I had not been able to fix it due to the pain in my head.

All I could do as I sat in the Emergency Room was to cry out to God as I waited for the doctors to see me. I prayed, "Dear Lord, help me!" I believed that somehow He would. I remember thinking, "When will the doctors be available to help me, and why had I been kept waiting for so long?" That's when I heard the loud abusive outburst from one of the nurses at the desk.

"You people are all the same," she stated. She was speaking firmly and with a disgusted tone to another lady of colour who was having difficulty in supplying the required information. This scene was in full view of all the staff, parents and family members who were present, and loud enough for us all to hear.

I had worked as a nurse for over eighteen years, and I knew, even in the midst of the pain pounding in my head that this was not being done in an orderly fashion. I was trained to know that it is important to have the proper attitude and tone of voice when admitting an incoming patient who needs medical care and attention.

For a moment, my mind traveled back in time. I reflected on having lived for over thirty years in England where I had worked as a nurse for over eighteen years. I had known and heard of similar occurrences, in England, but this was America! Slavery had been abolished, Civil Rights protests and marches had taken place. Dr. Martin Luther King, Jr., along with many others had fought long and hard to help make people not focus only on our many differences, but to be aware of the equal rights of all mankind. Surely, this could not be happening in Savannah!! It appeared that racism was *alive* and well.

In spite of the pain I was experiencing in my head and before my husband could stop me, I felt led by the Holy Spirit to get up on my feet. I made my way across the room to the admitting desk. I spoke courteously, but with conviction to the nurse involved and said, "Excuse me, Maam, please don't speak to this lady like that. Ask her for the required information in an orderly and respectful manner. Thank you very much." A mighty hush became apparent in the waiting room. She glared back at me, but before she could respond, her colleague approached me.

"Would you like to come this way Mrs.?" she asked. I followed behind her into a small room and sat down in the offered chair. The nurse placed the cuff of the spigomonometer on my arm and proceeded to take my blood pressure.

I soon responded, "That's too high for me. You've pumped the cuff up too high." My upper arm was in extreme pain and my head now felt like it was on the verge of exploding. I began praying in tongues and hoped God would now intervene on my behalf. I very quickly passed out.

When I regained consciousness, I was surprised to be lying on a trolley (cot). A young man in a frantic state was trying to insert a cannula into a vein in my left hand. "Please clean my arm," I pleaded. Soon he found a vein and administered intravenous drugs into my body. Shortly thereafter, I lapsed into unconsciousness. Thank You, Jesus!

I was kept sedated and remained in the Coronary Care Unit at the hospital for three full days before becoming conscious. Of course during those three days, I had plenty to dream about. I spoke in tongues, and I felt that I was able to swim, dance and sing extremely well. (Anyone who has heard me sing knows it had to be under God's anointing). I know that the Holy Spirit was present, and indeed I felt loved and comforted, even though I did not know what was happening to me in the natural. In my heart and mind God birthed new ministries, and I received confirmation on others that were already established inside me.

As I awoke, I received this Word, "You serve a risen Savior."

When the doctor visited me during the next few days, he found me "clothed in my right mind". My pain had diminished and all remaining observations were satisfactory. We are still not sure what caused the sudden elevation in my blood pressure or the cause of my severe headache. I do know that I am extremely thankful to my Lord and Savior, Jesus Christ for snatching my body from the very jaws of death, and healing my body on this particular occasion.

Hallelujah, Thank you, Jesus for the great things you have done. I thank and praise Him.

I am alive today because of God's goodness, mercy and His love. He did not leave me or forsake me. I'm also thankful to all the doctors and nurses who cared for me, as well as my church members, family, co-workers and friends who prayed for me. I am a firm believer in the power of prayer. I am also thankful that the Lord gave me the boldness to speak on behalf of the young lady during that unfortunate situation with the admitting nurse in the Emergency Room.

I sincerely hope that she felt some comfort following my intervention. I am not ashamed of the Gospel of Jesus Christ, and choose to be obedient to Him as He leads and directs my paths.

My thanks for your time spent reading this testimony. May it enrich a portion of your life as we journey towards His Kingdom.

"You knit me together in my mother's womb, I praise you because I am fearfully and wonderfully made;" (Psalm 139: 13b-14 NIV)

My daughter, Brandyce, affectionately known as Brandy, is a healthy, happy, well-adjusted child, whose chances of survival on a frigid evening on January of 1985 were guarded. It was the eleventh day of January at 2:12 pm at Memorial Medical Center in Savannah, Georgia that I gave birth to my two months premature, two pounds-thirteen ounces baby girl during an emergency Cesarean Section. Nothing could have prepared me for the events that took place thereafter.

My husband and I planned this pregnancy after five years of marriage. I fully anticipated the healthy birth of my daughter. Six and a half months of following my gynecologist's instructions with meticulous care gave me an internal solace that I would indeed deliver a healthy baby.

Then it happened, so unexpectedly, and so untimely. I began to experience several unusual symptoms. These symptoms were not present during the prior six and a half months of my pregnancy. I experienced blurred vision, recurring headaches, excessive water retention, and an elevated blood pressure. A phone call to my doctor resulted in my immediate admittance to the hospital. I was diagnosed as having a condition called Pre-eclampsia. I spent a week and a half of intense bed rest. I was only allowed to lie on my left side to aid in stabilizing an ever- elevated blood pressure.

By mid-week, my condition worsened. I developed a condition called Albuminuria or Toxemia (the spilling of proteins in the urine). A fetal monitor revealed that I was in labor; however, the contractions were not strong enough for me to dilate. The monitor also revealed that my child was nearing a level of distress.

My physician warned my husband and me that the time had come when we needed to decide on whose life was to be saved if circumstances warranted such a decision-mine or my unborn child. My husband made the painstaking decision that my life would be spared. Although he wanted this baby as much as I did, his decision was formed around his being the father of three from a previous marriage. If worst came to worst, of course we would try again.

At that point, any semblance of hope was a mere illusion. Praying became more and more difficult to participate in. My spiritual steadfastness was waning. Why pray? Why hope? Just let it be over! My almost two weeks of confinement in the hospital, isolated in a private room was getting the best of me. I felt like a prisoner in solitary confinement. Occupational therapy was an option, but in no way a solution. I wanted my blessed event to happen.

On Friday, January 11, sixteen days before my twenty- seventh birthday, it happened. My gynecologist made his early morning rounds, and decided that the time had come when my daughter must be delivered to capture any hope of both her and my survivals. I notified my husband of the impending delivery.

By noon I was prepared for the birth of my child. I remember lying on my back talking to my friend, Carolyn, who sat with me while my husband left to make a phone call. Suddenly I felt a gush of warm water. Ignorantly, I believed I had urinated on myself. Later, I learned that my water bag had burst. A glimmer of hope emerged. My baby girl was about to make her debut.

As I was moved to the delivery room, several family members had gathered. My husband gave me a tender kiss on my forehead. I reminded him of the promise he had made to me regarding our child's gender. He had assured me before conception that our first child would be a girl. The last conscious thought I had before the anesthesia took effect, was the utterance of a silent prayer. I remember saying, "Lord, let *Your* will be done!"

I slept through the days immediately following Brandy's birth. I remember very little. I do remember making an abrupt move that caused me to grimace in pain. This pain I learned stemmed from the stapled vertical incision made in my abdomen to remove Brandy from the birth canal. I also recall my husband telling me that we were indeed the parents of a baby girl.

The snapshots I saw prior to seeing Brandy did not prepare me for the actual meeting. Brandy was born on Friday, but I did not meet her until the following Wednesday. My husband wheeled me to the Neonatal Unit— an advanced center filled with many life-saving mechanisms designed to meet the needs of ill newborn babies. I was awestruck by the sounds that echoed from all the machinery and the sight of so many sick babies. Meeting my daughter for the first time was frightening...I nearly fainted at the sight of her. She was so tiny! I could not discern how someone so small could survive.

There were intravenous feeding tubes protruding from her arms and legs. An oxygen mask covered her tiny face. Her eyes were covered with white patches. She wore no clothing. I barely touched her for fear that I would dislodge a tube. The attending nurse assured me that touching Brandy would not be life threatening. She further interjected that touching and holding her would indeed be beneficial. My fears were calmed when I began stroking my baby girl ever so gently. The "mother-daughter" bonding process took shape at that precise moment.

The following Friday, I was discharged from the hospital. I was happy to be going home. However, I was deeply saddened because I was leaving my little girl behind. What sustained me was my faith that God would heal Brandy, and soon she would be home with us.

Days turned into weeks, weeks turned into months. I maintained constant contact with the Neonatal Unit via telephone calls and visits. I began to take an active role in Brandy's feedings. She ate every two hours. During the day and some nights, I was at the hospital to feed her. Special permission was granted to my husband and me to visit past visiting hours.

It was a painful ordeal to witness Brandy gain weight, only to loose it. The formula prescribed for her gave her severe stomach pains. This resulted in constant and violent regurgitation. By then, anger had set in. Yes, I was an angry mother! I was angry with God.

I remember getting into my car, driving aimlessly. I could no longer bare the sight of the Neonatal Unit...all the sights and sounds made my senses numb. While driving, I cried out to the Lord. I remember scolding Him for putting my baby through this ordeal. I found myself constantly asking Him, "Why me?" I thought that perhaps I was being punished for wanting a baby girl so badly. Or perhaps, some misdeed from my childhood had come back to haunt me.

After trying several different formulas, Brandy was finally able to tolerate one. The violent regurgitation ceased. Her weight began to stabilize, but then a blood transfusion followed. Her condition steadily improved. She was transferred from Memorial Medical Center's Neonatal Unit to Candler Hospital's Progressive Care Unit for Infants where she remained for one month. Her condition continued to improve. She was free of all the tubes and wires that once adorned the monitor. They were replaced with soft pink night-gowns and sleepers. One of her caretakers had placed a pink bow in her soft hair. The nametag on her isolet no longer read "Baby Girl" instead it read "Brandyce". The God I serve is a healer, and He had proved himself faithful in healing Brandy.

As a rule premature babies were only released to come home after gaining five pounds. An exception was made, and Brandy was discharged to come *home sweet home* after tipping the scales at four pounds and twelve ounces.

Many valuable lessons were learned from this ordeal. I learned through this ordeal that God will meet you where you are. In spite of my anger towards Him, He did not leave or forsake Brandy or me. It was amazing that as my anger *decreased* Brandy's weight *increased*. As Brandy's weight *increased*, my faith in God was *strengthened*.

I further learned that "Without faith it is impossible to please God, because anyone who comes to Him must believe that He exists and that He rewards them that earnestly seek Him."(Hebrews 11:6 NIV) God taught me that faith "is the substance of things hoped for, the evidence of things not seen." (Hebrews 11:1 KJV)

I had so hoped that I would be able to bring my little girl home free of tubes and machines. In time, the Lord allowed me to do just that. However, I realize now that God had an appointed time when Brandy would be released from the hospital and allowed to come home.

Although Brandy's birth was premature, there was *nothing* premature about God's grace and mercy. If Brandy had been released when *I* wanted her to be, the tubes would have accompanied her, and I don't think I could have coped with that. God was *faithful* enough not to even have me put me to the test. I learned that my thoughts are not God's, for His thoughts are higher than mine are.

The greatest lesson I learned was that in order to have a testimony, one must have a test -a test of strength, faith and courage. Now, because of this ordeal, I know for myself that God's Word is true.

"...and Jesus healed many who had various diseases."
(Mark 1:34 NIV)

My most challenging experience occurred in November 1994, when I contracted a rare illness known as Gullain Barre´ Syndrome. This disorder causes the Milan to disappear from all the nerves in the body, causing total paralysis. Initially, my eyes would not close, even when I slept.

My primary physician told me that the illness itself is not fatal; however, the complications could cause death. He assured me that all of the doctors who were consulted were taking every precaution to keep complications to a minimum. My challenge was twofold. First, I needed to have confidence in my medical caretakers. Secondly, I needed to keep faith in the Christian principles that had always controlled my responses to situations in my life.

I never imagined that I would find myself in a battle for dear life. I had full control of my mind, yet, paralysis made it impossible for me to move, and the respirator made it impossible for me to speak. Day in and day out, I would lie in the same hospital bed, unable to share my thought with those around me. No one could hear me but God. He became my confident, my comforter, my enabler, my peace-giver, my heart fixer, and my mind regulator. Each day I would lie there and wait patiently for His healing touch to repair my broken body.

Recovery was slow, but steady once movement became possible.

I began receiving physical and occupational therapy almost immediately upon diagnosis. The nine doctors, nurses, various physical therapists, plus respiratory therapists worked diligently with me physically and psychologically. By January 1995, I began projecting my dismissal date from the hospital and my return date to work. I was really overjoyed when I was moved from the ICU to PCU in mid January. At the end of January, I was moved to the Rehab Unit, and began a rigorous program of learning to walk and write again. Unfortunately, my penmanship did not improve; however, there is a positive. My signature remained the same and that was good for banking purposes. On Valentine's Day, I was told that I would be released the next day. Outpatient rehabilitation would be terminated the next day. I received outpatient services during the month of March, and I returned to work on April 1, 1995. It was very exciting to return to work!

This experience has given me a deeper sense of appreciation for health care professionals. It has also given me more love for my family, friends, pastor, ministerial colleagues, and above all for God! I felt the presence of my heavenly Father throughout the illness and during the long road to recovery. I have always spoken of the almighty power of God, the loving presence of Jesus, and the comforting indwelling of the Holy Spirit. Nevertheless, the concepts that were learned through study and teaching of the Holy Bible became reality when I had to hold on to every promise found in that Holy Writ. My most challenging experience has taught me that all things are truly possible, if we only *believe*. I know that God has the *power* to deliver us from anything, if we have the *faith*.

Chapter 4

TESTIMONIES OF PROVISION

"For I know the plans I have for you, declares the Lord, plans to prosper you and not harm you, plans to give you hope and a future." (Jeremiah 29:11 NIV)

I am approaching the age of fifty and have faced many of what I call *valley of the shadow of death* experiences in my lifetime. These situations have often been emotionally exhausting, and sometimes seemed to have no way of escape. I can truly say that each situation and outcome is a testament to the mercy, power, and faithfulness of God.

This *valley of the shadow of death* experience began ten years ago when the agency that I had worked for almost twenty years was in financial trouble and had to reduce its work force. Colleagues that I had virtually grown up with started being laid off without much warning. All of us were filled with uncertainty—each day we went into work could have been our last. Though I felt apprehension like everyone else, knowing that God had brought me through other *valley* situations gave me confidence that *somehow* I would survive this one too. Because I have a personal relationship with Jesus Christ, I believed He would intercede on my behalf with God, the Father. I held on tightly to my faith that God is ultimately in charge.

I survived the first round of layoffs, because I had been moved to another department within the agency. God was even in *this* working on my behalf (but I couldn't see it at the time.). The agency did not settle into any state of stability, and the employees worked daily under the stress of not knowing if the agency would ever become solvent again.

Months passed and I was offered an opportunity to apply for a position that would take me away from the building. I would be working on a collaborative contract with another agency. I could not understand why this offer was given to *me*, because I felt that I was a *good* employee. Nonetheless, I hurriedly submitted a resume. Prior to this *valley* situation I found myself in, I had never had to submit a resume or interview for a position. Now, I found myself in the position of hurriedly getting together an updated resume and then interviewing for the position for two days.

In addition, my former supervisor informed me that our department was being scrutinized by an ever-changing administration, and that some personnel changes would occur to help boost productivity. At that point, I must admit that I became nervous, because I was up against stiff competition for a job that I knew nothing about, and I did not have the academic credentials for. However, I was offered one of three positions. (God was with me again, but I was clueless of His intervention).

Sadly, there were several more reductions in the workforce during my almost three years away from my home agency. I was truly grateful that my salary and benefits remained the same while I was stationed at another site. However, this arrangement ended when the host agency cancelled without warning the contract before its completion. Again, I found myself falling into the *valley*! I was assured that the termination of the contract was not a reflection of my job performance, and was offered an opportunity to *apply* for the same position by program administrators. I interviewed and was offered the job with one week to accept or decline.

I returned to my home agency and immediately began to get the run around. Needless to say, I understood that because of the termination of the contract, the agency did not have an obligation to place me in another program position. Unfortunately, no one ever informed me that I was not given a permanent job assignment. Neither could anyone assure me that my job was secure. This was a *deep valley* that had no way of escape that seemed right .The options all seemed to have their own evil outcomes. If I quit the agency, I would lose all of my years toward retirement, current salary, and benefits. If I stayed, I would pass up a steady job that unfortunately included a substantial cut in pay along with benefit changes.

I felt ill equipped to make such a life changing decision in my own strength or through the counsel of family or friends. Therefore, I did the *only* thing that I knew would help; I prayed and asked God for guidance. During my times of meditation and prayer the Holy Spirit guided me toward scriptures that helped calm my spirit and sooth my grief.

I believe that God was building me up to make a decision that He had already ordained.

I remembered that God is always with me no matter where I go, and that He knew me even in my mother's womb, because He fashioned me in the secret place. (Psalm 139:13). We had a long -standing relationship. I remembered that God has a plan for me that included a future and a hope (Jeremiah 29:11). I remembered that He orders my steps and something good would come of this situation (Romans 8:28) because I loved the Lord and he has a purpose for me. I remembered that God is my refuge, my strength and my strong tower. I remembered that the steps of a righteous man are ordered by the Lord (Psalm 37:23), and that He would hide me beneath his wings (if He chose) from my enemies (Psalm 17, Psalm 46). I remembered that I could abide in the shadow of the Almighty (Psalm 91). Moreover, I remembered Job and God's faithfulness to him- Job's losses… and his restoration.

Ultimately, I put my faith into *action*, and chose to work for the agency that offered me a secure job. I submitted a letter of resignation to my old agency, because I was to start immediately in the position that I had accepted. I was relieved that I had made that choice when three days later I received a "reduction in force letter". (This time I could *see* God's intervention). I am still grateful and thankful to God for his protection and guidance during this *valley of the shadow of death* experience. Since that time He has continued to bless me and has opened *so* many doors of opportunity for me… far more than I could ever ask or think.

Affirmation

I am blessed and highly favored of the Lord,

And I will not be denied the *power*, the *future* and

The *hope* that God has planned for me.

Therefore, I Will:

Lay aside *every* weight of my own vain imaginations,

The fiery darts of the enemy, and the
Scornful mocking doctrine of men

That seek to destroy me—to keep me separated from the

Love and Will of God.

"And my God will meet all your needs according to His glorious riches in Christ Jesus."
(Philippians 4:19 NIV)

There have been so many situations in my life when I have been down to my *last* something: my last dollar, last pair of stockings, last bit of gas, or my last hope. It would be dishonest for me to not to say that sometimes I have become so discouraged that for a *moment* I just wanted to give in. However, in each situation I have faced, a still small voice within me would ask, "Now what can *you* do?" In every instance, sooner or later, this question would turn my mind away from the *impossible* and redirect my thinking towards the *possible*. Suddenly, I would remember that I had put some money in a secret place, or my son would need the van and put some gas in it. I may be inspired to write a grant proposal, or I may just be led to certain passages in the Word that seemed to *speak* directly to me about the situation. Each time I became encouraged and my faith grew. Without fail, the Word would build me up emotionally and spiritually and fortify me with faith to face whatever obstacle lay before me. Each time I had to make a conscious *decision* to place my trust and confidence in God's ability to supply my need and ultimately work the situation out for my good. Then I had to *listen* and *wait* for His guidance.

Sometimes my old enemy, *pride*, would raise his ugly head and bring along with him his companion, *shame*, to entice me into isolating and not revealing to anyone what I may really have been going through. However, I have learned through my *walk* with God that sometimes not only may I have lost a blessing, but I may have robbed someone else of their opportunity to be a blessing *to* me. God will often bless us at the point of our need by allowing someone to be a channel through which He pours us a blessing. Wisdom has taught me that God's ways are not like my ways, and I try hard *not* to question His methods, though sometimes it isn't easy.

When I dedicated my life to Christ, I did not know that sometimes things would be so *hard*. They were hard because I was used to being in what I thought was *control* and *reasoning* everything from my intellect. Solutions that I would come up with would often wind up being *quick fixes* that were not able to endure for the long haul. However, I have learned that when God gives me a solution, though it may cause my flesh to *suffer* for a while, it is perfect. God is interested in perfecting my character, and this means scraping away old habits and thinking patterns. Sometimes it *hurts*.

As I have learned to surrender my self-will, which has always been *very* strong, to God's perfect will for my life, I have learned to *let go* and *let God* have His way. The Word of God admonishes us to, "Trust in the Lord with all your heart and lean not on your own understanding; in all your ways acknowledge Him, and He will make your path straight." (Proverbs 3:5-6 NIB)

I have also learned that sometimes when man says, "No." God will say, "Yes" in spite of the odds that may seem against you. I remember a time when my van was seven years old and had over 176,000 miles on it. It needed a rebuilt transmission that would cost $1,400.00. I didn't have the finances and my credit status was poor. I needed a van not only for my job, but for my ministry work as well. I was in a dilemma. However, the Word tells us that we *have not* because we *ask not*. I prayed and placed my petition before the Lord. I knew that *He* knew I needed good reliable transportation.

As life would have it, I owed only $500.00 more to pay off the van. My intellect told me, "You know you can't afford to get into more debt, and you probably won't qualify for a loan." For a while I would entertain those thoughts until I would hear the familiar still small voice urge me to,

"Fear not, trust in the Lord and be anxious for nothing. I know what you have need of."

The Word says to "seek and you will find." Eventually with the encouragement of my oldest son and the support of a prayer partner, I set off in *faith* to *seek* a vehicle. She and I drove over forty miles to another state that was unfamiliar to me. Along the way I noticed a sign that had two men with huge smiling faces advertising a Chrysler Dealership in the city where we were headed. I felt a *check* in my spirit (a kind of knowing that it may be a *sign* from God) directing me where to go. We missed the turn to the dealership my prayer partner had suggested I look, and wound up right in front of the Chrysler Dealership that had been on the sign. I chuckled to myself and told my friend, "That's just like God; I'd better stop here first." I felt compelled to go in. I have learned that God's ways are not like ours, so I let His Spirit guide and direct me. "In his heart a man plans his course, but the Lord determines his steps." (Proverbs 16:9 NIV)

Sure enough, there I found just the van I wanted with all the features I needed at a great price. I learned that the manager of the dealership was a Christian, and he worked on my behalf by giving me over $3000 trade-in for my van, and paying the remaining $500.00 I owed on it as well. Then came my time of faith. We were there a few hours, and I knew they were trying to find financing. The salesman said they were having trouble getting through. I knew he *really* meant getting my *credit* through. Anyway, he suggested we go home and he'd call. The whole while my prayer partner and I stood in faith praying and believing that God would supply my *need* and bless me with that particular van.

I drove back home in my old van feeling somewhat disappointed, yet my *faith* told me that the van was mine. On the drive home, a still small voice said over and over— "Delay does not mean denial." I held on to these words. I arrived home and picked my daughter up from school. I had hoped I would drive up in a new van to surprise her. However, it didn't work out that way.

I got undressed, took a shower, put on fresh clothes and just resigned myself that I wasn't going to worry, because God had things under His control. Then the phone rang and the salesman said, "Come on out and get your new van." I was ecstatic as I quickly told my daughter to get ready because we were going to pick up our new van.

When we arrived, the van had been freshly washed and waxed and looked brand new. It was two years old and had 40,000 miles on it, but it was new to me, and I knew it was a gift from God. For the next few weeks, I received notices from lenders saying that they were sorry they were not able to give me a car loan. I just collected and saved them as testimonials of God's mercy and grace. Again, man had said "No", but my heavenly Father said, "Yes!" God is my provider and He will *always* supply all my needs according to *His*, not my, riches in glory!

**"Beloved, I pray that you may prosper in all things and be in
health, just as your soul prospers." (III John 1:2 KJV)**

According to the *Thorndike-Barnhart Dictionary*, the term *challenge* may be defined as: a contest, a dare, or anything that
requires much effort to overcome or continue. During my lifetime, I
have encountered many situations that seemed too difficult for me to
overcome. Yet, with the help of God, perseverance, and hard work I
survived! I am certain that if the average person reflects over his
past, he or she would agree that overcoming one challenging experience prepares us with skills to be victorious over the next battle.

The most significant part of my story begins with the loving
bond that developed between my grandmother and me as I was
being reared in a household of three generations consisting of my
grandmother, my parents, my brother and me. During that time, I
spent countless hours with my grandmother who was both loving
and nurturing.

When I was four years old, my parents, my infant brother and I
relocated to a rural community on the outskirts of Cincinnati, Ohio.
This was during World War II, and my father worked in the Steel
Mill. Since there was a shortage of men in the workforce, my
parents decided to return us to my grandmother's care, (which was
not unusual in those days) so they could both work and save money
to buy a home.

The return to my maternal grandmother was great; however,

three years later granny and I waged *war* when my dad wanted to reunite the family in Ohio permanently. Reluctantly, my father awarded custody of me to my grandmother. My brother returned to my parents.

I attended St. Mary's Catholic School from grade two through eight. I was relatively healthy with the exception of Whooping Cough, which lasted for an entire month. I was a good student and an easy child to manage.

I attended Sunday school and church every Sunday morning and A.C.E. League every Sunday evening. It was mandatory to attend Mass on all midweek holy days of obligation or we did not get an "A" in Religion. We prayed four times daily in school: before school, before and after lunch and just before dismissal. Grandmother and I would have prayer at 6:00 a. m. each morning and at bedtime. Whenever we had a petition before the Lord, I read the 4th Psalm three times before sun-up, and recited the 23rd Psalm in my heart each time I thought of the petition daily. We were also taught to make a three or seven day Novena (light a candle, drop a dime in the area under candles and pray) to add penance to prayer. My claim to fame was, "I am 50% A. M. E., 50% Catholic and 100% Child of God!" One thing I learned from both my grandmother and Catholic school was the importance of prayer.

When I was promoted to the twelfth grade, I expressed a desire to go to college. The fact that I received a college education was a miracle. When I shared what I desired to do to earn a living, my grandmother insisted that I major in Elementary Education. I desired to major in Social Work. Her argument was that there would always be children to teach; however, she was not sure about the need for social services.

The miracle of the college degree began to transpire as the high school seniors were preparing for Honors Night. As grandmother and I discussed college, I mentioned the lack of funds. Grandmother reminded me of the times that God put food on our table plus provided for rent and utilities. She said, "My Father is rich in houses and land, He alone holds the wealth of this world in His hands. I will fast and pray. The Lord will make a way for you to get a college degree."

The next day, one of my teachers, Mrs. Margaret Law, sent for me to report to her class. After questioning me regarding my plans for the future, Mrs. Law informed me that I would be the recipient of the Sigma Gamma Rho Scholarship on Honors Night. This paid my tuition for my freshman year of college.

My sophomore year was financed with funds acquired by my ironing tubs of clothes, tips acquired from being a curbside waitress at Ben's Spot and working in the Sidney A. Jones Florist.

As my junior year approached, it seemed more difficult to acquire the $40.50 each quarter, so I began to discuss dropping out of college. Old Hattie Murray (my grandmother) would hear nothing of the sort. She fasted, prayed, and sang a popular gospel song of that period entitled "Just Tell Jesus". Grandmother then conferred with Fred and John Wright, my paternal uncle and cousin, plus Lillian Murray, my maternal aunt.

Following a stern lecture from these three relatives plus a commitment of tuition for one quarter from each of them for the next two years, trusting in God, and working hard work, I overcame that challenge and was awarded a Bachelor of Science Degree in Elementary Education in June 1958. I worked as an elementary classroom teacher for two years. Marriage and children interrupted my career for a season.

When I returned to the work force, I was employed as a social worker with the Department of Family and Children Services for many years. I returned to college to obtain a Master's degree in social work with financial assistance from an educational program offered by DFCS. Through the program, the Department would financially assist me in obtaining my MSW degree, if I would agree to repay the agency by working two years for each year of college tuition. Again, the Lord made a way for me. In 1970, I was awarded a Master of Social Work degree. After graduation, I worked at DFCS the required time necessary to repay the educational assistance I had received from the Department. I continued to work there as a social worker until I returned to the Board of Education as a school social worker. So as the Lord would have it, my grandmother and I *both* got our wish. I became a teacher *and* a social worker. Through those experiences, I realized that Philippians 4:13

is a true statement for "I can do all things through Christ who strengthens me."

Upon overcoming each challenge, I experienced the feeling of exuberant joy, happiness, and gratitude to Almighty God for all those human resources that He activated on my behalf.

"In his heart a man plans his course but the Lord determines his steps." (Proverbs 16:9)

I am indeed a living testimony! God has been so good to me over the years that I just praise and thank Him for being God all by Himself! Each stepping stone He allowed me to encounter in my life was all part of His plan to take me to another level in my faith walk with Him.

He watched over me, guided and protected me during my years at Florida A & M University. I was indeed blessed to have the opportunity to go to college, as many of those whom I knew were not afforded that chance. There were many times when I probably should have been dead and sleeping in my grave...but God kept me for a greater purpose.

After graduation, God allowed me to have jobs that, by man's standards, I was not qualified to have. For example, when I applied for a HIV/AIDS Case Management position with a mental health center and health department. The position was with a pilot collaborative project, and management was seeking a person with at least a Master's Degree. I was the *only* candidate without a Master's Degree. However, because I *am* the righteousness of God, He commanded His angels to move on my behalf, and bless me, so that I could have the position and be a blessing to others. I was selected for the position. I live by the motto "Service to others is rent for our room in Heaven."

Each day, I thank God for allowing me to excel in the areas that man said I could not excel. I came to the agency where I am currently employed as the Executive Director as the Assistant Director. After working here for a year as the Assistant Director, the Executive Director left. The Board of Directors was faced with finding someone to fill the Executive's position. As the Board debated about whether I was a suitable candidate, one member did all in her power to have me *not* appointed to the position. She literally cried in that meeting, because she did not believe that I was suitable to the handle the task of being the Executive Director of such an agency. However, my steps had already been ordered by God. *He* placed me here as the Executive Director to be used as a vessel and mouthpiece for *His* plans for the agency to be fulfilled.

I thank God for health, strength, family, friends, co-workers, and the community I serve. Above all, I thank God for giving me wisdom and understanding to get through life's tough twists and turns. And when the storms of life are raging, I thank God for giving me peace that passes all understanding. That peace guards my heart and mind in Christ Jesus.

Thanks be to God!

Chapter 5

TESTIMONIES OF PEACE IN THE MIDST OF THE STORM

"And the peace of God which passeth all understanding, shall keep your hearts and minds through Christ Jesus."
(Philippians 4:7 KJV)

I was married at nineteen, the mother of two at twenty- two, and a single parent at twenty- five. I thank God who has always been foremost in my life for my blessings (in spite of me), and my two sons, who are the love and joy of my life.

When my sons were about eleven and twelve years old, the devil put the thought in my mind, "Now that the boys are older and you have instilled good values in them, it's alright for you to take time for yourself." So I began going out, meeting people, and slowly becoming a part of the world. It started with Happy Hour, and then it progressed to the Saturday nightlife of partying. I began to gamble— everybody was doing it. I played bingo and numbers, but after a few big wins at the Dog Race I was hooked. It was once a week- sometimes twice. A day at the Dog Race even became a Saturday outing for my boys and me. I stayed ahead of the game, because the devil knew, I would not continue with anything that I didn't see as *profitable*. I had to have funds to take care of my children and maintain my elaborate party life.

But then one day, Jesus came into my heart. He *asked* me to examine my life. I did examine it, and realized that the life I was living was unfulfilling. The only time I could remember feeling *really* fulfilled was when I had been living for God. That was the day

He picked me up and turned me around! I began cleaning up my life for God, and by 1998, I had made changes in my life that I believed were pleasing to God. Though not perfect, I steadily strived (at a great pace) towards God's will for my life. I started attending church regularly and got involved. I was determined to live for God, and Satan knew there was *no* turning around for me. However, unbeknown to me, the devil had begun a strategy of attack on my sons.

It became evident to me that he was using my children in an effort to shatter my world, and turn me away from my contentment in God. In addition to things like struggling with my youngest son to complete his education and to become matured; I had to face his becoming a single father. His first child was born on May 8, 1998. Then on August 9, 1999 the FBI arrested my oldest son. He had been involved in 13 robberies including one bank.

Years before when my sons' father was not there for them and refused to pay child support, I turned to God. I had prayed and asked Him to be my sons' earthly as well as heavenly Father. When my son was arrested, I needed God to help me understand *why* He allowed something like this to happen. Why didn't He reveal to me what was going on with my son? I turned to the Word for answers. There, I found the strength and peace to walk through this storm in my life.

When my son was arrested, I felt lost. I was shaken, and turned to my family, friends, and even the church. Although they comforted me and sympathized with me, *nobody* could take away the pain. I turned to God. I talked to Him like I never talked to Him before. Oh, we had a *time* throughout this trial. It seemed that God would not allow *anyone* to be there for me. He used this situation to draw me closer to Him and to help me learn more about Him.

One of my most vivid memories during this trial in my life was while I was visiting my son in the county jail. I sat down and was waiting to be called for my visit. The man seated beside me who had been drinking greeted me. After greeting him, he said that God wanted him to tell me that "He was bigger than my circumstance." The man went on to tell me more about God's goodness. This conversation happened at a time that I *needed* to hear a word from God. You never know *whom* God is going to use to speak to you.

I asked the gentleman about his situation, and why he was still of the world (doing things out of the Will of God). He began to talk about the story of Jonah and how he was *running* from what God wanted for him too, but that he loved God. I encouraged him to change his life, because I believe God wants to use him. He said that one day he was going to turn his life around. It was a profound experience.

I gained strength from God and was able to go through court, and eventually deliver my son on February 7, 2000 to the Coleman Federal Correctional Institute. My son was given a seven-year minimum mandatory sentence, even though it was not stated in a plea agreement that he had signed. He was not even told by the judge at his Rule 11 hearing (where the court determines whether the defendant understands the plea and that he signed it of his own free will) what the plea was. My son was supposed to be sentenced according to the Federal Sentencing Guidelines which meant he would not serve more than fifty- eight months. We have appealed and petitioned for an adjustment, but we have not been successful. I am still trusting in God and believing that the enemy will not prevail.

Through it all, my son has set his mind on Jesus and has drawn closer to God through studying the Word, praying, and believing that God is with him, even while he is in prison. He is studying drafting and is currently involved with a Youth at Risk Program at the facility. During this incarceration period, he has had time to think about what he did and what he hopes to do with his future.

My testimony is not ended in this situation, because I *believe* that God is going to deliver my son from his physical incarceration. I thank God he was never spiritually imprisoned because he was *free* to pray and worship God. Through this trial, I believe that my son is being refined. Although it has not been easy, God's Word says, "All things work together for the good of them that love the Lord and are called according to His purpose." (Romans 8:28KJV).

As a result of my son's experience, I have begun a small prison ministry, writing letters to other inmates, telling them about the goodness of God, and giving them encouragement to have hope during this trial period in their life.

After that situation, the devil tried other tactics to turn me around. For example, one day when my youngest son was trans-porting some friends home from work (he picked them up and took them home each day), he was involved in a tragic car accident. One of his friends lost his life. Another friend was hospitalized for months. It was hard on us all, especially my son, because he was driving. However, God showed up and showed out at the scene of the accident when a lady driving by got out of her car, formed a circle of love around my son and me, and began to pray. God continued to be with us even when others wanted to blame my son for the death and hospitalization of his friends. Through this storm as well, God was with us and gave me *peace.*

This is my prayer:

> "Forgive me, I was of the world, but thank you, Father, that I am now *in* the world not *of* it, and living *by* the Word.

> Forgive me, I *was* conformed to the world, but thank you, Father, that the Word has *now* transformed me.

> I started out life with the joy of motherhood. I found my delight in my sons' childhood.

> I gave love, because I was taught love.

> Somehow along the way I lost my sight, but thank you God for now I see the light.

> All I want is for You, Father, to have your way in my life." Amen

"You will keep in perfect peace him whose mind is steadfast, because he trusts in you." (Isaiah 26:3 NIV)

Seven years ago, I had to face going through a storm during which I had to really put my trust and faith in God. My husband, who operated his own tree removal service at the time, had a serious accident on a job site. He fell thirty feet from his bucket, and was in intensive care for ten days, and hospitalized for five months.

I had to turn a deaf ear to the question that kept coming in my mind, "What will I do if my husband does not survive?" However, my trust in God and my personal relationship with Christ, enabled me to find the courage and strength to step in and become the family leader. I took care of the business, our home, the mounting bills, traveled thirty miles one way daily to visit my husband, took care of my active daughter with Down Syndrome, and provided comfort and encouragement to our teen-age son. Though I, myself, was barely hanging on with little sleep and much anxiety, I clung to my faith and trust in God's ability to "lead me beside quiet waters and to restore my soul." (Psalm 23:2 NIV) I poured myself out to God many nights during that long recovery. I refused to believe that we were walking "through the valley of the shadow of death" so I clung to God's *Hands*, and "feared no evil, because He was with me." (Psalm 23:4 NIV).

My husband has undergone thirty-seven orthopedic surgeries

over the past seven years. Even though he was often in excruciating pain, he never missed an opportunity to witness to nurses, physicians and therapists about the healing love of Christ. In spite of his own pain, the Holy Spirit gave my husband the grace to share the Good News of God's love and mercy with the people who were caring for him. He in turn drew strength from them as "goodness and mercy followed him." (Psalm 23:6 NIV) This amazed us all. It strengthened my faith, our family's faith, and the faith of those who cared for him.

This experience brought our family closer together. Through it, we learned to appreciate each other, the miracle of life, and the power of prayer. We trusted God for my husband's very life, and believed God had a plan for our family. We trusted in the faithfulness of God to heal, and we never lost hope!

It is essential when you are undergoing trials to hold on to your faith and belief that "Nothing is impossible with God." (Luke 1:37 NIV) Staying positive, especially when you are going through trials, is a powerful witness to others of the power of prayer and God's great love to *carry* us through the storms of life.

I have learned through this experience that *everything* we have comes from God. If we understand and realize that we are *powerless* without God, then we have true humility. My husband's accident taught me humility. I remember that after a long night of worry, my husband undergoing eleven hours of surgery, and my sleeping in a cramped hospital waiting room, I awoke to see a magnificent sunrise over the city of Boston. I remember thinking, "Wow! God really is in charge!" Although my life had just been completely turned upside down, and time seemed to stand still, *yet*, here was a brand new day. The sun *still* came up! This gave me the freedom and ability to put my husband *completely* in God's hands and trust Him for the outcome. What a relief to know I was *not* in control!

Chapter 6

TESTIMONIES OF GOD'S FAITHFULNESS

"He refreshes and restores my life-my self; He leads me in the paths of righteousness [uprightness and right standing with Him]." (Psalm 23:3 Amp.)

When I was asked to be a presenter at a Cursillo I felt too imperfect, flawed, and human to be considered a leader, let alone get up in front of an audience and talk about being one. A Cursillo, which started in Spain in the 1930's, is a retreat designed to bring one closer into a personal relationship with Christ. It was the words of the popular hymn, "Here Am I, Lord", that helped me understand the simplicity of leading. I needed to remove my own ego from the equation. In the song, Christ asks, "Whom shall I send?"

The answer: "Here am I, Lord. It is I, Lord. I have heard you calling in the night. I will go, Lord, if You lead me. I will hold your people in my heart." I realized that as long as I am trusting that Christ will lead me, even in that endeavor, I could relax. All I needed was the willingness and a little time, effort and love.

I have been called bossy, stubborn, and controlling at times, but I have never considered myself a leader. However, I have heard the call of Christ, and I replied, "Here I am, Lord." Consequently, the Lord has used me as an instrument to lead my family and friends to Christ. We all have talents, (God given gifts), regardless of our positions in life. It doesn't matter if we are married or single, rich or poor. What does matter is how we use the abilities we possess. We are called to live a life in union with God and spread it to others.

God never asks the impossible of us.

Jesus said, "Come...follow Me." He has gifted us with the tools that we need to lead. He asks us to reach out and touch those around us and take our place as leaders. For me, being a leader sometimes means doing the inconvenient, sacrificing time and talent to do my best for Christ. The more I allow the Holy Spirit to control my life, the more effective a witness I become for Christ. The most important thing to me is to be a true friend of Jesus...to follow Him and know that He is truly present in my life. I believe I must always strive to trust in God for my life and the lives of people I love. And I have been tested in several areas to do just that.

I am married, and after my son, Sam, was born, my husband and I tried desperately to have another child. Discouraging infertility work-ups proved ineffective. After two surgical procedures, I had given up hope of becoming a mother again. Around this time, I went to a healing service, and was slain in the spirit for the first time in my life. Two months later, I found myself joyfully pregnant. We were so excited! We believed that it was truly a miracle!

By summertime things got "hairy". I went into labor at twenty-one weeks. After a difficult bed rest pregnancy, and a life threatening delivery, on December 1, 1999, we became the proud parents of a 7lb. 12 oz. full term baby girl! We named her Rachel Rose...Rachel, after the Biblical figure that suffered the loss of her children, and Rose, after St. Theresa, "The little flower". Rachel was beautiful and perfect. She had ten fingers and ten toes. We fell in love with her at first sight. However, the news that she had Down Syndrome caused me to shed *many* tears. My tears were soon turned into dancing by the firm belief that God had a marvelous plan for our lives.

Rachel has taught us patience and to trust in God's grace, faithfulness and mercy. She is now twelve years old and has exceeded all our expectations. She is bright and witty, and brings Jesus to everyone she meets! Just the other day while I was on the telephone with my brother who is a recovering alcoholic, and newly sober, I lost my temper with him and began to raise my voice. Rachel was apparently listening, and she looked up at me and stated very calmly, "Mum, God is in my heart and He *tells* me to be kind and peaceful. He is in your heart too, mum, but you can't hear Him because you're *yelling*." What's that expression? Out of the mouths of babes...!

"From the lips of children and infants you have ordained praise." (Matthew 21:6 NIV)

"Because of the Lord's great love we are not consumed, for His compassions never fail. They are new every morning; great is your faithfulness." (Lamentations 3:22-23 NIV)

I am a fifty- nine year old married mother of two children living in Massachusetts. I have been saved over thirty years. The Lord has really shown me and helped me to understand through many years of ministry that we all have a place in the body of Christ and a place in ministry. The things that we have experienced in our younger lives in our walk with God are footprints. In a lot of areas, we who are older are trailblazers. As we meet younger women, who are "pulling their hair out" over a particular situation, we must realize that if God has already walked us through that place or area, then it is our job to *pour* ourselves into another person or woman and share our deliverance.

God doesn't allow us to go through anything that is a test or trial to be wasted. This is where our testimonies come from- a test. When God delivers us and brings us over onto the other side, we become stronger, and we get to a place where we *know* God in a specific area. Then I believe it is our duty to *share* that experience with another person to give her *hope*. "Likewise, teach the older women to be reverent in the way they live, not to be slanderers or addicted to much wine, but to teach what is good. Then they can train the younger women to love their husbands and children, to be self-controlled and pure, to be busy at home, to be kind, and to be subject to their husbands, so that no one will malign the word of God." (Titus 2:3-4 NIV) As I minister to younger women, and share with them how God has been faithful to bring me through various trials in my life, they find strength and hope that they too can overcome their challenges with God's help.

God touches people through people, and the only way we can touch this world is one person at a time. When we look at the world situation and look at the spheres of influence, we realize that God places us in people's lives for certain lengths of times for certain reasons. He has a *goal* in mind. God wants us to demonstrate the same love He has for us with someone else. "A new command I give you; Love one another. As I have loved you, so you must love one another. By this all men will know that you are my disciples, if you love one another." (John 13:34 NIV) Recently, I personally learned through a situation with a good friend that when someone hurts your feelings, even if you are in the right, you have to forgive, even as God forgives us. Because we demonstrate God's love through our forgiveness, we must always be willing to forgive.

I am grateful that the Lord has allowed me to live as long as I have, and to look as well as I do. He has taken care of me, even when I thought the roof was going to cave in as I went through different situations. I have learned that God is really faithful. He has *always* proved Himself faithful in my life. I want women everywhere, young women and older women to know that with Christ in your life you can make it!

When the Lord saved me, I had just come out of a marriage. I got married to my first husband when I was very young. He committed adultery, had a child and all of that, and we broke up. I was in my early twenties and I thought my life was over. I had a son who was about two years old at the time. I didn't think that I could live without this man, and I decided that I couldn't go on. But the Lord stepped in!

I had it all set up: I had opened up the oven door, and turned the gas on in the stove, and laid my son down for a nap. I thought we would just drift off. Then I heard someone banging at my door. I got up to let her in. I thank God for being faithful in my life. He rescued me, even when I did not want to be rescued. That's the faithfulness of God! Through this and other experiences, I have found God to be a faithful friend.

My present husband has been out of work for about a year and a half, and there were days when I did not know which end was up, but God has provided us with what we have needed. He is faithful! Recently, He blessed me, not my husband, with a new job that I'm really not qualified for. God may not come how you think He will, but He will come. God is faithful to "supply all your needs according to His glorious riches in Christ Jesus." (Philippians 4: 19)

I just pray that these few words will provide encouragement for someone. Never ever let go of God's hands and take time in His Word and in prayer. As the old hymn goes, "Oh, what peace we often forfeit. Oh, what needless pain we bear. All because we do not carry, Everything to God in Prayer." I have found prayer to be the key. If you cast all your cares on Him in prayer, and spend time in His Word, you will grow closer to Him, and He will become the center of your joy. Let God be your first thought in the morning and your last thought at night.

I would encourage any woman, no matter what your age, to spend time in His Word, so that your spirit man can grow and mature. "I have hid your Word in my heart, that I may not sin against You."(Psalm 119:11) Pray my strength in God that He will help me to be the woman of God He has called me to be in these last days.

"The Lord is my Shepherd, I shall not want." (Psalm 23:1)

As early I can remember in my childhood, the 23rd Psalm was my constant prayer. I needed it for strength and reassurance to help me endure the various times I experienced pain and suffering in my life. It was my *comfort* when I couldn't *see* the green pastures or the still waters. Yet, I had faith, even as a little child, that God would be with me.

This scripture is my testimony of two significant and similar relationships that I have experienced in my life. One was my relationship with my *earthly* father, Pops, and the other with my *heavenly Father*, God.

I learned early in my life that my earthly father loved and praised God more than anyone else I knew. He relied on God for guidance throughout his lifetime. I was close to my father, and thought if he felt this way towards God, then it was okay for me to feel that way, too. Therefore, I began to develop a close relationship with God myself. "Fathers, do not exasperate your children; instead, bring them up in the training and instruction of the Lord." (Ephesians 6:4 NIV)

As I grew up living under Pops' rules and doctrines, I realized that life wasn't going to be easy. In an effort to be an obedient daughter and to please my *earthly* father, I tried to adhere to his rules as best I could. I followed the commandment, "Children, Obey your parents in the Lord for this is right." "Honor your father and mother"—which is the first commandment with a promise—"that it may go well with you, and that you may have long life on this earth." (Ephesians 6:1-2 NIV)

The positive relationship I shared with Pops made it easier for me to transfer to my confidence in him into a positive relationship with my *heavenly* Father, God. However, I have discovered again, that as I've tried to live by God's rules and commandments—it *isn't* easy. Yet, I strive daily to do those things that are acceptable and worthy in His sight. I am a living witness that when parents "Train a child in the way he should go, and when he is old he will not depart from it." (Proverbs 22:6 NIV) Very often when children are raised under Christian teachings, though they *may* stray for a while, usually, they will return to the ways of God.

Psalm 23, verse 4 reminds me that "I shall fear no evil for thou art with me." Verse 5 says, "Thou preparest a table before me in the presence of mine enemies." (KJV) These scriptures have given me comfort and peace in situations when I was afraid. Just knowing that my Father was with me was enough for me to be able to face whatever lay before me.

Yes, I can testify with certainty that through my life with my *seen* father, Pops, and my *unseen* Father, God, my faith in my heavenly Father is *everlasting*. And I will dwell in the house of the Lord forever.

"Let us hold fast to the profession of our faith without wavering; for he is faithful that promised."

The above scripture entered my spirit as I began to make preparation to share my testimony of the faithfulness of the Most High God.

The experiences that we encounter are not always understood at the time they are happening in our lives. However, we must hold fast to our faith in God knowing that He is faithful who has promised, and He will reveal His purpose in due time.

God entered my life at a very early age, but in my 30's a yearning for a more genuine relationship with Him developed in my heart. One day as I was doing my household chores, a strange feeling came upon me, and I cried out to the Lord, "I want to be a Christian in my heart." At that time I did not know what was happening to me.

The next day, I found myself in a "battle" that I did not have weapons or ammunition to fight.

I did not realize that my request would cause a *war* within my spirit— but it did. I was attacked spiritually by the enemy, and I did not know how to fight against him. Yet, I believed that my Redeemer would not leave me alone. Even as I cried out in my vexed spirit for relief, I experienced continual attacks from the enemy, but I believed God was with me. The attacks continued as the enemy tried to diminish my confidence in God. The devil threw fiery darts at my mind for months. However, I was able to continue my daily routine by the sustaining grace of God.

In the meantime, I shared this experience with ministers, family members, and friends, but no one seemed to understand what I was experiencing. I could not pray in my natural tongue (language), but the faithful God gave me another tongue that the enemy did not understand, so I could communicate with Him.

One day God led me to a book I had in my home entitled, *"Strengthening Your Faith"*. I opened the book and read it. The Lord of my salvation revealed to me through reading it what a *wilderness experience* is. It explained how a believer goes through a wilderness experience or conversion experience. John 3:3 Jesus says, "I tell you the truth, no one can see the kingdom of God unless he is born again." It helped me better understand what I was going through. It reminded me of Jesus' encounter with Satan when the enemy tried to tempt Him. The attacks did not stop after I read the book, but Jesus did not forsake me. He continued to reach out to me in my spirit and let me know that He was fighting the battles, not me.

Another day Jesus allowed me to hear and talk with a 700 Club member on the telephone that was familiar with spiritual warfare. She gave me a weapon to use when the enemy attacked my thoughts. She told me to rebuke the devil in the name of Jesus. I began to use those words on the attacker. Gradually, the attacks stopped, and my mind was returned to peace again. God's Word is true—we must be *born again*, that is of the Spirit. God kept me and proved Himself faithful to His promise. He did not leave me alone, and He safely brought me through the wilderness.

Praise be to the Most High God.

Chapter 7

TESTIMONIES OF DELIVERANCE

"Many are the afflictions of the righteous; but the Lord delivers him out of them all." (Psalm 34:19 KJV)

I believe with all my heart in the family. I am married and have three sons to whom I am devoted. I recently celebrated my twenty- fifth wedding anniversary with a beautiful renewal ceremony. I take my wedding vows seriously, and believe them to be a covenant among God, my husband and me. Make no mistake, not all of my days have been sunny, but one thing I can say without any wavering is that God is *faithful*. God has been the *cement* that has helped us endure the many challenges and trials that we have faced in our marriage and as parents. He has never forsaken or left me out on a limb! When I needed Him most, He's been right there making a way out of no way— time after time! Oh, He may not have come when I expected, but He was never late.

There have been several incidents in my life that involved my two oldest sons in which God has intervened. Because they are young Black males growing up in the southeastern part of the U. S., they are almost on an *endangered species* list. Small towns are nice places to live and raise your children if you are the *right* race. Even if you come from the right side of town, have graduated from high school and college, and are a practicing Christian, if you are a young Black male driving alone late at night, you may be in danger of being a prime target for Satan and the penal system.

Nevertheless, God is faithful. Even through man may say "No", you can't take what man says, as the final word. For only God is *Alpha* and *Omega*. I have learned that you cannot take what people say for granted. You have to deal with everything in the natural as well as the spirit realm. Consequently, as an African American mother dealing with Black males, I have learned not to accept anything at face value. I have also learned you must be spiritually discerning when facing situations involving your children.

Take, for instance, an incident that I went through with my middle son who recently graduated from college. When he was on his way home from work late one night, the police stopped him and said he was speeding. When they ran a check on his license, it showed that his license was suspended. He was arrested and incarcerated for driving on a suspended license.

We were told that we would have to pay $850.00 in order to get him out. My son told the authorities that his mother didn't have that kind of money, and asked them what other options were there. He was told that if he had some land he could get what is called a "property bond". Most people probably don't know about this kind of bond. If you have land, the sheriff can agree to use that as a way of getting someone released on bond without having to pay out of pocket money. Because we happened to have a parcel of land, we were able to use it as collateral for the bond, and paid no money.

Through faith, perseverance, and prayer, God intervened on my son's behalf, and very quickly turned this situation around. The officer that the information went out through said it had all been a mistake. A letter was written and sent out (which I still have a copy of) to the State Department letting them know that my son's license had *never* been suspended, and it had been a mistake. Just imagine what might have happened if we had not taken the stand to look into the situation more deeply to see what was going on. That child could have either had to spend time in jail until his court date, or we would have had to pay out a bunch of money for something that *never* happened. In this situation, God was faithful and intervened. We prayed for His help, and then followed His guidance. This was not the first time or the last that I have had to deal with the law.

Many times I think some people stereotype African American males and put them all in one category. Some people feel that they're the ones that break the law most of the time, and so consequently, if a crime has been committed then they must the perpetrators. I would say to all mothers and grandmothers, "Don't take things at face value." You must get to the bottom of things to discover what is *really* going on. Of course you really cannot do that unless you allow the Lord to lead, guide, and direct you, because He knows *all* things and will bring things hidden in darkness out into the light.

Recently, my oldest son was stopped for speeding and locked up for ten days due to an old probation violation. I was told that this was a situation in which he could not get a bond until he had served the required time. Well, man may have said "No", but God said, "Yes". It all happened so supernaturally that even the attorney, who we were able to get by the grace of God, was aware something unusual was happening. Initially, the attorney had said he could not take the case unless he got his money up front. Then he changed his position and allowed us to make payment arrangements. When he looked into the situation at first, he said that he didn't think he could get my son out on bond. However, the Lord showed him something there too!

Normally, in order to get a bond, you have to have a bond hearing. In this situation, my son didn't even have to have one. By the time I arrived in town to go to what I thought was a bond hearing, the Lord had already moved and turned the *heart* of the court system. The bond had already been set *without* a hearing. Everybody told me that it was one of those cases in which it could not happen— but it surely did. This shows you how awesome God is! If I had just sat back and gone on the basis of what I had been told, my son would have missed out on starting a class for college, and may have lost the scholarship he'd been provided with to go. His life could have taken a totally different turn.

By keeping my eyes on Jesus and doing what He instructed me to do, we were able to get my son released on bond, because we still hold the mortgage to a house in Savannah. Although the house has really been a financial burden for many years, God used it for such a time as this to be a blessing and a part of the solution for my son's release. Again, God worked on our behalf, so we were able to get the bond that everyone told us we could not get. It is certainly true when God says "All things work together for good..." (Romans 8:28 KJV). He means it!

"Let no one be found among you who sacrifices his son or daughter in the fire, who practices divination or sorcery, interprets omens, engages in witchcraft, or casts spells, or who is a medium or spiritist or who consults the dead. Anyone who does these things is detestable to the Lord, and because of these detestable practices the Lord your God will drive out those nations before you. You must be blameless before the Lord your God."(Deuteronomy 18:10-13 NIV)

I have always been a curious person who never liked surprises, because I always wanted to know what was going to happen. I also had a fascination with the supernatural. All these elements added together spelled *danger*.

I was raised in a fundamental Christian home by two devout Christian parents who lived by the Word. However, our teachings did not emphasize that the Holy Spirit is a *living* part of the Trinity (Father, Son, Holy Spirit) who was sent by God to help guide and lead us, even now. I was taught that the supernatural gifts ended at Pentecost, and now we have the inspired Word of God, the Bible, as our only guide. This is partly true, because in (Acts 2:38-39 NIV) Peter replied, "Repent and be baptized, every one of you, in the name of Jesus Christ for the forgiveness of your sins. And you will receive the gift of the Holy Spirit. The promise is for you and your children and for all who are far off-for whom the Lord our God will call." This implies that it was for those then and for those who were to come in the future. I had always had an ability to *know* and *sense* things about situations and people that I know *now* was a gift of *discernment* given to me by God. However *then*, because of my ignorance, I was attracted to the supernatural world of the occult.

The word "occult" sounds ominous, but people dabble in it unwittingly every day through reading their daily horoscopes, even playing numbers based on scriptures given out during Sunday church services, or talking to psychics over the telephone. I, like so many others, merely wanted to *know* what the future held. I remember that as a kid, I always want to be a gypsy at Halloween. I didn't know then that Halloween was honoring demons and was an anti-Christ celebration. Because my church did not condemn Halloween, I did not know it was not pleasing to God for it to be celebrated by Christians.

When my mother recognized my fascination with the supernatural, she warned me to stay away from any involvement with it, and that it was not of God. However, as I grew older, and more *worldly*, I just thought she was being old fashioned, overly worried, and just wanted me to stop from *knowing* what the future held. Oh, how I wished later that I had obeyed her. If I had, I would not have been drawn deeper and deeper into the realm of the occult by going to tea leaf readers, palm readers, tarot card readers, reading horoscopes and believing their predictions for my life. Little did I know that I was opening the door of satanic influence to invade my life.

Though I was baptized at the age of twelve and had accepted Christ, I did not receive the baptism of the Holy Spirit which is crucial for followers of Christ. It is through the guidance of the Holy Spirit that Christians are led into all truth. Satan knew that I was born to be a leader of men, and he pulled out all the supernatural tricks to seduce me to serve his kingdom of evil. For a season, I had lost my way and was seduced and deceived by the father of deceivers, the devil. But thank God for His grace and mercy. *He* had *created* me before I was formed in my mother's womb to be a leader. My birth name, Geraldyne, means "leader of the troops." I had always hated that name, but *now* I see even then, God's Hand was on me. "Before I formed you in your mother's womb I knew you, before you were born, I set you apart; I appointed you as a prophet to the nations." (Jeremiah 1:3 NIV)

My innocence and curiosity could have been my downfall if it were not that I had received Christ at any early age, and *greater* was He that was in me, than he that was in the world. As I grew in my Christian walk and in the Word, I learned that only God's Holy Spirit is the real guide. I John tells us, "Dear friends, do not believe every spirit, but test the spirits and see whether they are from God, because many false prophets have gone out into the world. This is how you will recognize the Spirit of God; every spirit that acknowledges Jesus Christ has come in the flesh is from God, but every spirit that does not acknowledge Jesus Christ is not from God. This is the spirit of the antichrist, which you have heard is coming and even now is already in the world. You dear children, are from God and have overcome them, because the one who is in you is greater than the one who is in the world." (I John 4: 1-4 NIV) Thank God for His Word that takes us out of darkness and puts us into the marvelous light of truth.

I praise God that when He sees one of His children over his or her head in trouble, like a devoted parent, He'll come down and rescue him or her. That's just what He did for me! He sent a friend who was saved and filled with the Holy Spirit to talk with me about Satan and the occult. She told me how he can influence even Christians into thinking that it is okay for them to dabble with new age thinking, etc. She prayed for me, and led me to pray a prayer of repentance and deliverance. I could actually feel the shackles begin to *pop off* in the spirit realm. Oh, they did not want to leave, but she kept pleading the Blood of Jesus against any satanic influences. In His name there is *all power* and all demons must flee. I shed a bucket of tears filled with shame and guilt. I asked God's forgiveness for every act of divination I had participated in whether consciously or subconsciously. I renounced all forms of the occult and pleaded the Blood of Jesus over each one. I asked His Holy Spirit to dwell in me and cover every place where there had even been the slightest trace of evil. I also asked forgiveness for all those who I may have led astray by enticing them to become involved with any occult practices.

God's timing is perfect, and my *curiosity* led me this time to search the scriptures for myself. I did not want to sin against God in this manner ever again. I pledged to God that I would go back and confess to each person that I had misled that Jesus Christ is the true Lord and Savior and only His Holy Spirit can guide and lead us. Further, I destroyed all books, symbols, charms, horoscope and zodiac wall hangings, so that they would not be a temptation to anyone else.

Now I understand that the supernatural realm is *real*, and it can be used for either good or evil. If you do not have a solid foundation in the Word of God, you can be deceived. It is crucial that you receive the baptism of the Holy Spirit, so that you will be better equipped to know how to fight against the devil and become aware of his tactics. If you have not received the baptism of the Holy Spirit, stay away from the supernatural altogether. Satan counterfeits all the things which God has created for our good and perverts them to be used for his evil purposes. God has given each of us gifts to be used to help build up the body of Christ. "Now to each one the manifestation of the (Holy) Spirit is given for the common good. To one there is given through the (Holy) Spirit the message of wisdom, to another the message of knowledge by means of the same Spirit, to another faith by the same Spirit, to another gifts of healing by that one Spirit, to another miraculous powers, to another prophecy, to another distinguishing between spirits, to another speaking in different tongues, and to still another the interpretation of tongues. All these are the work of one and the same Spirit, and He gives them to each one, just as He determines." (I Corinthians 12:7-11 NIV)

Parents, be wary of what you allow your children to read, especially books that may introduce them into the supernatural or magical realm of wizardry such as the Harry Potter series. Though some may say the books are harmless or even that they are well written, the reality is that they open young impressionable minds to the notions of potions and witchcraft which are abominations in the sight of God. Parents, it is *your* responsibility to protect your children from everything that even has an appearance of evil. "Finally, brothers, whatever is true, whatever is noble, whatever is right, whatever is pure, whatever is lovely, whatever is admirable-if anything is excellent or praiseworthy-think about such things." (Philippians 4:8 NIV)

Today, I am grateful for my deliverance from the devil's grasp. Now I am a warrior in God's army. I take advantage of every opportunity presented to me to proclaim the real power that only comes through the sacred Blood of Jesus Christ. Only by receiving Christ as our Lord and Savior can we be saved from sin, and set free to live life more abundantly. Jesus came to set the captives free from darkness and sin. He freed me, and He can and will do the same for you. First, you must recognize that you have sinned against Him by being involved with the occult and ask for His forgiveness. Next you must repent and be willing to turn away from all occult practices like reading your daily horoscope, no matter how innocent they may seem. It is vital that you renounce all forms of the occult that you have been involved with. Here is a list of some: palm readers, tea leaf readers, Ouija boards, crystals, numerology, horoscopes, zodiacs, psychics, wizardry, roots, casting spells, tarot cards, using scriptures for numbers to play, entertaining familiar spirits (those who are dead who may come in dreams), seances, etc.

"So I say, live by the (Holy) Spirit, and you will not gratify the desires of the sinful nature. The acts of the sinful nature are obvious; sexual immorality, impurity and debauchery (indecency); idolatry and witchcraft; hatred, discord, jealousy, fits of rage, selfish ambition; dissentions, factions and envy; drunkenness, orgies, and the like. I warn you, as I did before, that those who live like this will not inherit the kingdom of God." (Galatians 5: 16,19-21 NIV)

"He who dwells in the shelter of the Most High will rest in the shadow of the Almighty." (Psalm 91:1 NIV)

Sister Mariah and I have been friends for over twenty years. We haven't always agreed on everything, but that's what real friendship is all about. A good friend will tell you when you are wrong, and praise you when need it too. She has done both. I hope that these few words will help edify my sisters in the faith.

I have had a painful life and lots of hurts. Who hasn't? But through it all, God has been faithful to me. God delivered me from some of the things, and others He went through with me. Nevertheless, either way I came out stronger.

I've learned a lot about others and myself. Most of all I have learned that *I* am the person I can change. I cannot change *anyone* else. I've learned to keep my eyes focused on the Lord. You see I had the *super saint syndrome.* Perhaps you have met her, *super martyr*, the woman who says, "Yes" to everything. It never occurred to me to say "No".

Today, I have chosen the better part, which will not be taken from me. Jesus spoke to Martha when she was complaining about doing all the work while her sister, Mary, sat at His feet to listen and learn. "Martha, Martha," the Lord answered, "you are worried and upset about many things, but only one thing is needed. Mary has chosen the better, and it will not be taken away from her." (Luke 10:41-42 NIV) However, I didn't choose it by myself. After two heart attacks, God healed my heart, and surgery was not necessary. The doctors found a blockage; it showed up on the x-ray, but after several more tests and another x-ray, the doctors found *absolutely* nothing wrong. My faith and the Lord's power healed me. He gave me a new heart!

I was diagnosed with diabetes…that surely got my attention! Now, I am out of the driver's seat, and He (God) is in total charge of my life. All of the things that I *want* to do, or think I *can* do have come to a complete HALT! I now live one day at a time, and let everyone else do the same. I don't allow *any* demands to be placed on me, and I have learned to say, "No." I found out that "No" is a complete sentence, and that I don't have to feel guilty when I say it… "No". The more I say it, the easier it is becoming.

I have learned how to *rest* in God, how to trust Him, and depend on Him for everything! I now spend quality time with God, a place of settling, where my soul can be nurtured and encouraged to grow. Becoming who God created me to be is also very important. And though it has taken me over five decades to get there, through it all I have found out Jesus is *enough*. I don't have to do *all*, or be *all* anymore. Jesus loved *me* enough to die for me, and that's more than enough.

I am trying to achieve a sense of balance in my life instead of always trying to please others by saying, "Yes". I strive to say what is appropriate for the situation, and according to the condition of my schedule or my soul. Balance in a Christian life can be hard to come by. The problem is that we usually fall prey to one of two extremes. Either we put ourselves *first* and slip into spiritual pride, or we put others *first* and plunge into self imposed martyrdom. Both extremes can be subtle self-deceptions under the guise of putting God first.

How do we really show our love towards others? By extending grace, compassion, understanding and caring. We love them without trying to *fix* them. We forgive them, and we affirm their attempts to seek God (not to be their god). We encourage them to keep on trying, even when they fail. We offer them hope, solace and comfort…Dare we do less for ourselves?

IN CONCLUSION...

When you have a dream in your heart or a vision of something that you desire to accomplish, do not disregard it as something that cannot be done or that you cannot achieve. Just like these women of vision, who chose to believe that what appeared to be in the natural impossible was possible with God's intervention, so can you!

When you feel discouraged, need direction and guidance read the scriptures daily. God's word is a "lamp to my feet, and a light for my path." (Psalm 119:105) It is important that you develop a personal relationship with Christ. This is generally accomplished through seeking Him. Early in the morning, before the "cares" of the day have confronted you is an excellent time. Even if you have to get up earlier than you would like to, the rewards are worth it. The Word says that "I love those who love me, and those who seek me find me." (Proverbs 8:17 NIV). In James 1:5 (Amplified) we learn "If any of you is deficient in wisdom, let him ask of the giving God [Who gives] to everyone liberally and ungrudgingly, without reproaching or faultfinding, and it will be given him." There is a condition, however. That condition is that you must have faith. Many times you may be required to have supernatural faith—the kind of faith that no matter what the current circumstances may indicate or what the doctor's report says— you believe without a shadow of a doubt that God is more than able to accomplish whatever it is that you need.

You must doggedly hold on to that faith, even when others around you may try to discourage or try to make you doubt. James goes on to tell us in verse 6, "Only it must be in faith that he asks, with no wavering— no hesitating, no doubting. For the one who wavers (hesitates, doubts) is like the billowing surge out at sea, that is blown hither and thither and tossed by the wind." Do not allow your thoughts to vacillate back and forth-maybe I will...maybe I won't, maybe I can...maybe I can't. You must block out these thoughts and focus on the truth of God's promise that "Everything is possible for him who believes." (Mark 9: 23 NIV)

It is also important that you spend time daily in prayer. Prayer is simply talking to God. You don't have to pray with eloquent language or with lofty words. Just simply talk to God as you would if He were sitting right beside you. Remember He is your friend. You know how easy it is for you to talk and share your feeling and concerns with a dear friend. There is no better confidant or friend than Jesus is. The best thing about Him is that He is never too busy, too tired, or unavailable. He is always ready and willing to hear you. As the old hymn goes, "Have a little talk with Jesus. Tell Him all about your troubles. He will hear your faintest cry, and He will answer by and by..."

When you pray, always remember to thank God for what He has already done, what you believe that He will do. Praising God is important. He likes to know that we appreciate Him and what He has done for us, just as parents want to be appreciated by their children. Then lay your petitions or requests before Him. However, remember that He may not answer when you think He should, or in the way that you expect. Only know without a shadow of a doubt that His timing is always perfect, and His ways are beyond finding out— but perfect for every situation. Sometimes it may seem that He is not doing anything about your situation, but just know that He is faithfully working on your behalf. One thing I have learned is that you must have patience and wait! If you make a decision or move too soon, you may miss out on the real blessing that God has for you. If He tells you to wait on the corner of 5th Street for a purple truck which will hold your blessing, do it! Don't get tired and leave because just when you leave, the truck may be turning the corner, and you'll miss your blessing. Remember that obedience is better than sacrifice.

Also it is important for you to realize that we are in spiritual warfare. I have learned that the devil is defeated when you speak the Word of God against his attacks on you. Praying the *Word of God* and reciting scriptures are powerful *weapons* against the *darts* of the enemy. I have found the following prayer to be very effective when you pray it in the morning before you begin your day and God will bless you with His grace:

Good Morning, **Father!**
Good Morning, **Jesus!**
Good Morning, **Holy Spirit!**

Heavenly Father, according to Your Word, I present my body a living sacrifice, holy and acceptable in Thy sight. (**Romans 12:1**)

Now, Father, I gird my loins about with truth. I put on the breastplate of righteousness, I shod my feet with the preparation of the gospel of peace. Above all, I take the shield of faith wherewith I shall be able to quench all the fiery dart of the wicked. And I take the helmet of salvation, and the sword of the spirit, which is the Word of God. (**Ephesians 6:14-17**)

And according to Your Word, the glory of the Lord is my rear guard. (**Isaiah 58:8**)

Now Heavenly Father, I praise you and I thank you for the armor you have provided for me to dress in this day. I am completely covered now, in the name of Jesus, according to Your Word, Father.

Upon Jesus I have built my life, my home, and my marriage, and the gates of hell shall not prevail against it. (**Matthew 16:18**)

You are my Shepherd, and I shall not want. (**Psalm 23:1**)

For You have supplied all my needs according to Your riches in glory, and I can do all things through Christ who strengtheneth me. (**Philippians 4: 19, 13**)

I cast down all imaginations and bring into captivity every evil thought. (**Corinthians 10:5**)

I cast all my cares upon You, for You care for me. I praise You for walking in Divine Health. (**1 Peter 5:7**)

For You are my God who healeth all my diseases. (**Psalm 103:3**)
And by Your stripes I am healed. (**Isaiah 53:5**)

I just praise You and thank you for my prosperity and good health, even as my soul prospers. (**3 John:2**)

For the joy of the Lord is my strength. (**Nehemiah 8:10**)

Father, I have prayed according to Your Word, and You have said You would watch over Your Word to perform it. (**Jeremiah 1:12**)

Father, Just rise up and live big within me today, for I am Yours, in the name of Jesus. Amen

(Thinking it doesn't work-You must claim it by the words of your mouth.)

Always remember: Every word spoken becomes a living thing-To *minister* or to *destroy*. (Proverbs 18:21. 6:2. 4:20-22)

Finally, be sure to get involved in a Christian church fellowship with sound biblical doctrine that believes and teaches that Jesus Christ is the risen Son of God who died on the cross for our sins, so that we might have a right to eternal life. Find a church fellowship that teaches Christ arose on the third day, and ascended to heaven where He sits on the right hand of God the Father. It is so important, as I have learned, first through the vision God gave me, and then through walking the road to righteousness, that you do not have to try to walk alone. God gives us other Christians to love, support and help us on our journey. Fellowship is important! It provides a means of check and balance as well. Sometimes we all need edification, Godly counsel, or constructive criticism to help us discern the perfect will of God for our lives. But be wary of becoming dependent on what others think or even prophesize into your life.

It is crucial that you develop and maintain your own personal relationship with Christ. You must learn to hear His voice, follow His unction, seek Him through the Word, and do not do anything until you have a peace about it. God is not a God of confusion and He will do things in decency and in order. If you don't know what to do...do nothing. Just wait until you have a release in your spirit. God will always speak to you in a way that you can receive whether it is through a scripture, a song, a book, or a stranger on the subway. You just have to be alert and tuned in to His prompting.

Walking with God is an adventure everyday when you totally surrender your life and will into His care. Each day, even in the midst of trials, there are blessings...if you choose to find them! Instead of looking at what you don't have or what you haven't accomplished yet, meditate on what God has already done for you. Remember His faithfulness to deliver and to bless. Most of all remember that without a test there can be no testimony. Always be ready to share with others what God has done *for* and *through* you. "They overcame him by the blood of the Lamb and the word of their testimony." (Revelation 12:11)

Hold onto your vision... and though it tarry-wait for it!

DO YOU HAVE A TESTIMONY TO SHARE?

As you read this book, you may have said to yourself, " I have a testimony of what God did for me in my life that would be a blessing to someone else." Maybe you have kept the experience locked up in your trunk of forgotten memories. Now is the time to share with others how God has blessed, delivered, healed, provided, and saved *you.*

Many people have gone through some incredible things in their lives both positive and negative in which the Lord has showed Himself strong. If you are one of those people why not share your testimony as a means of encouraging someone else? You don't have to be a writer. Just write down what the Lord has put in your heart to share. The Holy Spirit will do the rest! The testimonies will be used as evangelist tools to give others inspiration and hope. They will give others courage to persevere and increase their faith in God's ability to heal, deliver and prosper.

If you would like to have your testimony included in the upcoming book of testimonials, please e-mail me at Hairam77@aol.com for further information. It is time for the body of Christ to *speak up* and *speak out* for Jesus!

Printed in the United States
16908LVS00002B/1-129